AERIAL PIRACY AND INTERNATIONAL LAW

AERIAL PIRACY AND INTERNATIONAL LAW

by

EDWARD McWHINNEY

Professor of Law,
Director of International and Comparative Legal Studies,
University of Indiana, Indianapolis

SECOND PRINTING

A.W. SIJTHOFF, LEIDEN

OCEANA PUBLICATIONS, INC., DOBBS FERRY, N.Y.

1973

ISBN 90 286 0001 9 (Sijthoff)
ISBN 0-379-00038 (Oceana)

Library of Congress Catalog Card Number: 78-161940

THE INSTITUTE OF AIR AND SPACE LAW
McGILL UNIVERSITY, MONTREAL

International Advisory Committee

Professor Richard R. Baxter, Harvard Law School, Cambridge, Massachusetts, U.S.A.

Mr. Marcel Cadieux, C.C., Q.C., Canadian Embassy, Washington, D.C., U.S.A.

Professor Maxwell Cohen, Q.C., Faculty of Law, McGill University, Montreal, Canada.

Professor Huibert Drion, Faculty of Law, University of Leiden, Leiden, The Netherlands.

Sir William P. Hildred, C.B., O.B.E. Frensham, Surrey, England.

Judge Manfred Lachs, International Court of Justice, The Hague, The Netherlands.

Professor Oliver Lissitzyn, School of Law, Columbia University, New York, N.Y., U.S.A.

Professor Myres S. McDougal, Yale Law School, New Haven, Connecticut, U.S.A.

Dr. Eugène Pépin, Paris, France.

Mr. A. Beatty Rosevear, Q.C., Burlington, Ontario, Canada.

Dr. P.K. Roy, International Civil Aviation Organization, Montreal, Canada.

Mr. Oscar Schachter, United Nations Institute for Training and Research, United Nations, New York., N.Y., U.S.A.

Sir Francis Vallat, K.C.M.G., Q.C., Faculty of Law, King's College, University of London, London, England.

The Right Hon. Lord Wilberforce, Lincoln's Inn, London, England.

5

Institute Faculty

Director of the Institute: Edward McWhinney, Q.C.
Professors: E. McWhinney, I.A. Vlasic, H.R. Hahlo
Associate Professor: M.A. Bradley
Law Librarian: Miss Marianne F. Scott
Secretary: Miss Sheila F. Macbrayne
Lecturers (part-time): Gerald F. FitzGerald, Julian Gazdik, David I. Johnston, Nicolas M. Matte, James J. Smith

ACKNOWLEDGMENTS

These essays grew out of an international conference on the general theme — "Aerial Piracy and International Law"— held at the Institute of Air and Space Law at McGill University, Montreal, on Friday, October 30th, and Saturday, October 31st, 1970. The conference was held as a joint meeting of the Institute; of the American Society of International Law of Washington, D.C.; and of the International Law Association (Canadian Branch) and Canadian Society of International Law.

Those of the essays that were originally presented as conference papers have now been re-written for publication in book form; while, beyond that, several essays have been specially commissioned for inclusion in the present volume.

Our thanks are due to the American Society of International Law and its Executive Director, Stephen M. Schwebel, and to the International Law Association (Canadian Branch) and its President, Louis M. Bloomfield, for advice and encouragement and support in the planning and organisation of the conference. Beyond that, we are indebted to the Ford Foundation for its continuing support, throughout the past six to seven years, to the Institute and its activities.

Miss Sheila Macbrayne, Secretary of the Institute, has rendered invaluable assistance, going well beyond the call of duty, in the organisation of the conference and in the preparation of these essays for publication. In addition, E.A. Zussman (Ben-Yakir), LL.M. (McGill), and J.–C. Martinelli, LL.M. (McGill), have helped very amply in the editing of the papers for publication.

January 31st, 1971   Edward McWhinney
                                      McGill University, Montreal

CONTRIBUTORS

Bissonnette, P.A. Assistant Under-Secretary of State for External Affairs and Legal Adviser, Department of External Affairs, Ottawa.

Butler, Charles F. United States Minister-Representative to the International Civil Aviation Organisation, Montreal.

Clark, L.S. Legal Officer, Department of External Affairs, Ottawa; sometime Delegate to the ICAO Assembly and Alternate Representative on the ICAO Council.

FitzGerald, Gerald F. Senior Legal Officer, International Civil Aviation Organisation, Montreal; Lecturer (part-time), Institute of Air and Space Law, McGill University, Montreal.

Green, L.C. University Professor, University of Alberta, Edmonton, Alberta.

Lissitzyn, Oliver J. Professor of Public Law, Columbia University, New York.

McWhinney, Edward. Q.C.; Professor of Law, and Director of International and Comparative Legal Studies, University of Indiana, Indianapolis.

Pourcelet, Michel. Professeur à la faculté de droit de l'université de Montréal, Montréal.

Rhinelander, John. Deputy Legal Adviser, Department of State, Washington, D.C.

Valladão, Haroldo. Catedratico de Direito Internacional Privado das Universidades Federal e Catolica do Rio de Janeiro; Antigo Presidente do Instituto e da Ordem dos Advogados do Brasil.

9

TABLE OF CONTENTS

11

APPENDICES

13

14

Chapter 1

INTERNATIONAL LEGAL PROBLEM-SOLVING AND THE
PRACTICAL DILEMMA OF HIJACKING

by Edward McWhinney

Aerial piracy,[1] or,—to give it its special North American
title,— aerial hijacking, has been an international problem,
peculiarly, of the decade of the 1960s, beginning with the first
"Cuban" hijackings in 1961, and ending with the concerted
hijackings to the Jordanian desert and the ensuing orgiastic
destruction of the airplanes involved and with the minor rash
of hijackings or attempted hijackings of Soviet civil aircraft.
   Hijackings did not, of course, begin in 1961. There were
numerous, little publicised incidents, during the early Cold
War era, of the seizing or forcible diversion of military aircraft
from one side of the Iron Curtain to the other, possibly with
the tacit encouragement or aid of the military intelligence
units on both sides. There were also the occasional cases of
political refugees taking over or commandeering regular passenger aircraft and directing them on to a presumed political
haven. In the 1960s, however, because of the very frequency
of repetition of the incidents and because of what one might
call the mounting escalation of the political intensity of those
incidents and, in consequence also, the escalation of the disregard for, and gratuitous mistreatment of, the innocent
civilian aircraft passengers involved, the act of hijacking itself

   [1] Aerial piracy is, of course, a popular rather than a strictly legal term.
The limitations as to possible analogies from the international customary
law as to piracy or as to the application of the provisions of the 1958
Geneva Convention on the High Seas, are clear. See genrally Van Pan-
huys, Aircraft Hijacking and International Law, 9 *Columbia Journal of
Transnational Law* 1, at 4 et seq. (1970).

has begun to be recharacterised from an erstwhile occasional romantic adventure, to be written up as such in often admiring or laudatory terms in the popular press, into a genuine international delict.

The "Cuban" hijackings began innocently enough, at the opening of the 1960s, with a number of diversions of small aircraft and small ships from Cuba to the United States, by political opponents of the newly installed Castro *régime* who used the hijackings as a means of effecting their escape from Cuba. The means of conveyance of these Cuban refugees were, in certain cases, subsequently seized or attached by court order, in the United States, as a means of meeting unsatisfied legal claims by American citizens against the Cuban government or its instrumentalities. When the first United States civil passenger aircraft began to be hijacked to Cuba shortly thereafter, the Castro government, understandably enough perhaps, took advantage of the situation to extract a *quid pro quo* bargain with the United States government of a return to Cuba of any Cuban planes or vessels hijacked to the United States in return for the release of any American civil aircraft that might be forcibly diverted to Cuba. This *de facto* accord between Cuba and the United States appears to have been operated, with reasonable speed and smoothness, over the years; though in fact the hijackings now seem to be all from the United States and other Western hemisphere countries to Cuba, the opportunities for use of aircraft as a means of departure from Cuba, on the part of anti-Castro political refugees, apparently having dwindled away. It is also a fact that the Castro government, with one major exception only, made years ago in the case of Mexico, has consistently refused to permit the hijackers of such civil passenger aircraft to be extradited to the United States or other hemispheric countries for criminal prosecution arising from their hijacking acts; and, concomitantly, the Castro government has also signally neglected to prosecute the same hijackers under Cuban national law. In recent times the Castro government has been pressing an offer of a bilateral agreement or accord covering reciprocal undertakings of compulsory extradition of hijackers, with any country willing to make such an arrangement with it. It is

16

suggested that this Cuban offer, which is accompanied at the same time by a resolute refusal by Cuba to enter into any multilateral conventions on control of hijacking, may be induced by a desire to compel a United States' resumption of diplomatic relations with Cuba as the price of the United States' finally obtaining some effective measures for countering the wave of forcible diversions of American civil passenger aircraft to Cuba.

Though the initial hijackings of Cuban small aircraft to the United States, at the opening of the 1960s, seem to have been the work of genuine political refugees, and though no doubt some at least of the hijackers of American civil passenger aircraft to Cuba may also have acted under what they felt to be sincere political motives, in fact the predominant personality patterns emerging from the wave of "Cuban" hijackings have been those unstable, unbalanced individuals with disturbed domestic lives. Hijacking has thus become, in the Cuban context at least, essentially a form of direct physical outlet for the inner repressions and frustrations of pathological personality-types.

In the context of the Mediterranean and the Middle East, however,— especially after the resumed Arab-Israeli military conflict of June, 1967—hijacking seems to have developed merely as one means, among a number of available alternative, competing means, for trying to achieve political objectives without recourse to direct military action or military confrontation, with all the risks of a further disastrous defeat that any such military action might seem to involve. The advantages of hijacking, in this regard, as a weapon for achieving major national political objectives by non-military means, have been the unusually small expenditure of money and energy and lives that such action seems to have involved, up to date; the relative ease with which it has been able to be effected; the enormous international publicity for one's political programme that it has managed to engender; and finally, at least until the multiple hijackings to the Jordanian desert in September, 1970, the certain element of perverse sympathy that the hijackings seem to have evoked in many quarters, stemming no doubt from the superficial comparison of the physical

17

frailty of the hijackers themselves (especially the Palestinian woman commando) and all the accumulated power and prestige symbolised by the jets or jumbo-jets that the hijackers have succeeded in taking over.

A peculiarly unpleasant and repulsive side-effect of the Mediterranean and Middle Eastern hijackings, however, has been the visiting, by the hijackers themselves and, more importantly, by the governmental officials of the countries in which they have succeeded in forcing the hijacked aircraft to land, of the consequences of their over-riding political objectives upon the innocent passengers and air crew who, by personal ill-chance, happen to have found themselves in the aircraft at the time of its original armed diversion. These poor unfortunate passengers and air crew members have all too frequently been used, without pity and without mercy,—by the hijackers and by the governmental officials on the ground in the countries to which the hijacked aircraft have been forcibly diverted,—as helpless pawns in games of political blackmail and pression of a trans-national character. In the result, in jurisprudential terms, the air transport cluster of specialised legal rules, and the special values that they imply— freedom of movement and communication, untrammelled by arbitrary delays or controls and restrictions—have been sought to be subordinated by the political actors involved as principals in the hijackings, to other claimed or postulated special legal categories variously described as having to do with internal armed conflicts, wars of national liberation, privileged combatancy status, and the like.[2] In the case of the most recent attempted hijackings in the Soviet Union, it has been suggested that these two rival, competing groups of rules and principles — the air transport cluster and the asserted "new" international law cluster— may coalesce: persons or groups subject to religious discrimination or persecution in their home countries and officially denied the opportunity of leaving it of their own free will, according to this argument, may have a right to

[2] See Meron, Some Legal Aspects of Arab Terrorists' Claims to Privileged Combatancy, in Shoham (ed.), *Of Law and Man* (1971). And see also *The Law of Armed Conflicts* (Carnegie Endowment for International Peace (1971)).

18

vindicate that freedom of movement supposedly guaranteed under general international law, by hijacking aircraft if need be, if that be the only effective means of escaping the persecution that is available to them.[3]

The 19th century liberal democracy looked with special favour and kindness upon the political refugee, particularly where he had escaped from an authoritarian, tyrannical political *régime*. It is this special solicitude for the political offender, acting with a *bona fide* political motive, that explains that general "political offences" exception, established under so many Western national legal systems, to the granting of requests for extradition to face criminal charges abroad, and expressly inserted by many of the same countries as special clauses in bilateral extradition treaties mady by them with other countries.[4] And it also explains, in measure, the opposition by some of these same Western countries, coinciding of course with the attitudes of Cuba and the Arab countries which had, of course, a direct and immediate political interest in categorically rejecting any notion of an international law duty to permit extradition of criminal hijackers — to the insertion of any special clause in any proposed new multilateral convention controlling hijacking, requiring either the automatic extradition of hijackers on demand of any country wishing to assert jurisdiction over them, or else the choice between automatic extradition of hijackers for trial elsewhere and prosecution of them, instead, under one's own national laws.

The countervailing point of view — and it is the view, essentially, in Stammler's terms, of the legal "special community" constituted by the air transport industry and its officials and its clients and customers, — is that the free movement and interchange of men and goods over national frontiers is so vital

[3] See the letter to the Editor of the *New York Times,* by the U.S. Representative to the U.N. Commission on Human Rights, Rita E. Hauser, published in the *New York Times,* January 7th, 1971.

[4] See Sundberg, La piraterie aérienne, *Revue Internationale de Droit Pénal* 165, at 172 et seq. (1970); and see also Bassiouni, Ideologically motivated offences and the political offences exception in extradition, 19 *De Paul Law Review* 217 (1969).

to the efficient, everyday functioning of the contemporary World Community as to elevate the notion of freedom of communication to the rank of an *imperative* principle of international law,—something in the nature of contemporary *jus cogens*. Even the old Watchman's state, (so the argument goes), which did not believe too much in the attempt at regulation of society by legal means, regarded acceptance of the rules of the road – here, the ordinary traffic rules — as being basic.

The transportation and communication "special community" having, by definition, a special concern for the maintenance of the effective functioning and safety of the international civil air transport services, was naturally in the vanguard of the fight to control aerial hijacking once it had been demonstrated, — as it had, certainly, by the early 1960s — to be a serious social threat. This special community's never precisely defined or rigid ranks certainly included, at that time, the international inter-governmental organisation, the International Civil Aviation Organisation (ICAO); the international, private, inter-airline organisation, the International Air Transport Association (IATA); the large international airline companies themselves; and probably also the international airline pilots through their own special organisation (IFALPA). The special community probably did not, at that time, include, however,— to judge by the apparent apathy and indifference and dragging of feet with which they responded to even so innocuous a measure as the Tokyo Convention of 1963 — the various national air ministries in the main countries; and it certainly did not include then, as indeed it does not now, the consumers or customers—here, the fare-paying passengers who have of course never been effectively organised as a community pressure group.

Viewing the attempt at control of aerial hijacking by legal means as an applied exercise in international legal problem-solving, it must be conceded, at the outset, that the response of the legal special community concerned was substantially limited by its own very restrictiveness in terms of range and numbers of societal groups involved, and by the seemingly low priority that the individual national governments mainly con-

20

cerned with civil aviation gave to the freedom of transportation and communication in the early 1960s as a principle to be fought for in their international bargaining and give-and-take. Faced, then, with the practical dilemma of political choice between a comprehensively drafted multilateral convention that would really have teeth in it but which, presumably, would attract many fewer ratifications because of that; and a vaguer or more modest draft that might reasonably, on that account, be expected to obtain more ratifications, ICAO clearly opted for the second choice in bringing forth the Tokyo Convention of 1963. The harder-line American proposals for an affirmative obligation on the part of States in whose territory a hijacked aircraft might land to punish the hijackers, which had been present in the earlier Rome draft of 1962, were deleted altogether from the final text as adopted in Tokyo in 1963. In the end result what was left was a blending of the worst elements of the two alternative policy choices already adumbrated — a convention without teeth in it, and one with very, very few ratifications. Although only twelve ratifications were necessary to bring the Tokyo Convention into legal force, it took more than six years before, in December, 1969, the Convention finally became legally operative, the United States being the twelfth country to ratify.

It may even be argued that, so far as its substantive provisions go, the Tokyo Convention, in establishing as its most affirmative obligation for its signatories the duty to

"take all appropriate measures to restore control of the aircraft to its lawful commander or to preserve his control of the aircraft";[5]

and to

"permit its passengers and crew to continue their journey as soon as practicable, and . . . return the aircraft and its cargo to the persons lawfully entitled to possession";[6]

merely creates a legal pleonasm. Such an obligation already fully existed, it may be suggested, under customary international law, on the analogy of foreign vessels entering the port of another country, in distress. In seeking expresly to record such

[5] Tokyo Convention, 1963, Article 11(1).
[6] Ibid., Article 11(2).

21

an obligation in the case of a hijacked aircraft, in the text of a multilateral convention presented for general signature and ratification, it may even be that the prime movers at the Tokyo conference weakened that obligation from the psychological viewpoint, by giving rise to the implication that such an obligation was a new one which would not be binding on any state unless affirmatively accepted by it by signature and ratification of the Tokyo Convention. No other construction would seem rational if we seek to explain or justify in strictly legal terms the actions of countries like Algeria and Syria which consciously and deliberately held civil airline passengers and air crew and the civil aircraft themselves, for sustained periods of time after the aircraft had been hijacked to their national territory, — as hostages in ransom for satisfaction of national political demands completely separate from and irrelevant to the hijacking act itself.

Faced with the practical failure of international, intergovernmental responses by the multilateral convention or treaty route, and also the relative ineffectiveness of individual national, governmental responses to control anything other than hijackings wholly committed within their own national borders, the legal special community turned perforce to other, alternative forms of social control, since the social problem itself — hijacking of aircraft — showed no signs of abating. The potentially most effective such alternative form of social control, — this time through international private (non-governmental) action, — has perhaps been the proposal of the International Federation of Airline Pilots Associations (IFALPA) for a boycott by its members on flights into and out of any countries that fail promptly to release civil aircraft and their passengers and air crew hijacked into their national territory. After seemingly forcing an immediate and complete compliance by the national government concerned on the only occasion on which IFALPA policy has been fully invoked — the case of the El Al aircraft hijacked to Algeria in the summer of 1968 — this highly successful form of direct action has apparently been dropped, whether because of covert pressures placed on individual IFALPA members by their own national foreign ministries or by the airline companies that employed them, or because of doubt on the part of IFALPA members of the limits of their own personal legal liability.

The remaining major alternative form of social control has been the widely publicised group of national, private, non-governmental measures for safety inspection and security surveillance and control of civil aircraft and their passengers and air crew, both on the ground and in the air. While there has been a considerable degree of coordination and exchange of information, especially as to airport control measures, on the part of individual airlines, all this with the full blessing and cooperation of ICAO and IATA, the degree of diligence and enthusiasm will obviously depend on the individual airlines concerned. And the measures involved can probably, by their very nature, never expect to be fully effective or fool-proof.

The possibilites, then, of some really comprehensive community control measures emerging in relation to aerial hijacking, had seemed reasonably gloomy until the extraordinarily rapid succession of crimes of violence directed against aircraft, occurring in 1970. In February, 1970, bomb outrages were perpretrated, in flight, against *Swissair* and *Austrian Airlines* planes; and Switzerland and Austria, both major airline states which had not, however, been among the first twelve states to ratify the Tokyo Convention, moved politically to cause the convocation of an Extraordinary Assembly of ICAO in June, 1970, to try to deal with the aircraft sabotage problem. Again, the concerted hijackings to the Jordanian desert in September, 1970, the mass destruction of the aircraft concerned, and the particularly difficult circumstances in which the innocent passengers and air crew were held by their kidnappers, seemed to created a strong wave of indignation against the hijackers, in marked contrast to some earlier tendencies to try to romanticise hijackers as a group. Finally the Soviet hijackings, both the successful attempts and the aborted ones, produced, for the first time seemingly, a strong wave of indignation against aircraft hijacking, as such, on the part of the Soviet government and people;[7] and thus produced, for

[7] Bandit attack on Soviet airplane, *Pravda* (Moscow), October 16, 1970; *Izvestiya* (Moscow) October 17, 1970. Saving People's lives,

23

the first time also, a genuine community of interest in finding a solution to the hijacking problem on the part of the two main participants in the contemporary world power process, the Soviet Union and the United States.[8]

It would, of course, be an overly simplistic view of complex political events to view the enthusiastic participation by the Soviet Union in the conference at The Hague, in December, 1970, which finally gave rise to an anti-hijacking convention with teeth in it, on a purely *post hoc, propter hoc* basis —as, in effect, an angry Soviet governmental response to the shock of the Soviet hijackings of the preceding Autumn months. Any such interpretation ignores, of course, the fact that the Soviet Union had already moved to join the International Civil Aviation Organisation *before* the first Soviet hijackings took place, even though the administrative formalities as to joining were not completed until after that time.[9] Nevertheless, whatever the causes for the new Soviet policy in favour of affirmative inter-governmental action against hijacking, the fact remains that the happy coincidence of Soviet and United States attitudes paralleled that significant Soviet-United States bipolar support and underwriting and sponsorship for the other main ventures in international law-making in the era of Soviet-Western Coexistence and "Friendly Relations", since the Kennedy-Khrushchev *détente* was inaugurated with the peacful resolution of the Cuban Missile Crisis in October, 1962. We refer here, of course, to such major achievements in international law-making as the Moscow Test Ban Treaty of August, 1963; the Space Treaty of January, 1967; the Nuclear Non-Proliferation Treaty; and, not least, the bilateral, Soviet-United States step-by-step cutbacks in armaments in various key areas under what Premier Khrushchev called the "politic of mutual example."

Izvestiya, October 18, 1970. Legitimate demand, *Pravda,* October 20, 1970. We demand extradition of the criminals, *Izvestiya,* October 21, 1970.

  [8] Stop Air Piracy, *Pravda,* December 4, 1970.

  [9] The Soviet Union officially joined ICAO as from November 14th, 1970, thereby becoming the 120th member of ICAO. *Pravda,* November 28, 1970; ICAO (Montreal), News Release, November, 1970.

24

Whether, in spite of the joint Soviet-United States sponsorship, the new anti-hijacking convention adopted at The Hague in December, 1970, will receive general and widespread ratification and so become effective international law-in-action, remains to be seen. The real "teeth" in the new convention — the alternative requirement either of extradition of hijackers on request, or else prosecution of them under one's own national laws — may certainly serve to scare away from signature and ratification of the convention text some of the main protagonists in the politically sensitive hijackings of recent years — the "Cuban" hijackings, and the Mediterranean and Middle Eastern group of cases. The compulsory extradition provisions, even though posed on the basis of an alternative to criminal prosecution under one's own national laws, may also conceivably turn away some of the older, Western countries that traditionally have valued very highly the "political offences" exception to extradition proceedings.

For the first group of countries, — Cuba and the Middle Eastern countries, — the remedy of minimum social control may have to be achieved, perforce, by the slow, patient process of negotiating special bilateral agreements; with the hope that, in time, a network of such bilateral agreements may fill any gaps constituted by any really widespread failure to sign or to ratify the new convention against hijacking adopted at The Hague in December, 1970.

For the second group of countries, — those older, Western countries already referred to, — the hope will have to be that, in considering any "political offences" based request for exemption from extradition proceedings, the countries concerned will bear in mind the principle of proportionality and of the necessary balance between ends and means in any attempt, through hijacking, to achieve political refuge in another country. Under this principle of proportionality, already adumbrated in various national systems of jurisprudence, the court attempts to decide, on a pragmatic basis, whether or not the hijacker's objective of seeking to attain political asylum has been accomplished with proper regard for the lives and physical security of innocent passengers and air crew on the plane concerned. It is not, of course, a very satisfactory approach for those who accept the freedom of transport and communication principle as a paramount, imperative principle of international law; but it may have to serve, *faute de mieux* as the necessary minimum social control in the case of those countries still reluctant to embrace the more complete and comprehensive social control represented by The Hague text. The quick and enthusiastic response, up to date, in terms of actual signatures to The Hague text, on the part both of the main airline countries and certainly of those with the choicest landing rights to offer for purposes of bilateral agreements, suggests in fact that those choosing to remain, for various reasons, outside The Hague convention special community, may have very little to offer in terms of bargaining power. They may also be likely to be subject in the future to those international private, non-governmental economic pressures, of the type so successfully applied in the past by IFALPA, if their cooperation should ever need to be exacted in the interest of the World Community and of the freedom of transportation and communication generally.

Chapter 2

THE PATH TO INTERNATIONAL LEGISLATION AGAINST HIJACKING

by Charles F. Butler

The question of unlawful seizure of aircraft is probably the most important task that today faces the International Civil Aviation Organization and the world legal community involved in aviation matters.

It might be well from the outset to indicate the magnitude of the problem that is now facing aviation. It has been said that a relatively few number of people in percentage terms are affected by the problem of unlawful seizure of aircraft. Unlawful seizure is the phrase, incidentally, which I will use to mean the forcible diversion of hijacking of an aircraft. I will not use the phrase aerial piracy because it is generally considered that unlawful seizure of an aircraft is not in the strict sense of the word "piracy"; and it has therefore been felt desirable to develop another term which would be descriptive of the specific act. Conventions being developed at the present time label the act as "unlawful seizure" and I feel it best if we continue to follow that course.

So far as concerns the magnitude of the problem, in percentage terms the proportion of passengers, who have been directly affected by the unlawful seizure of aircraft, is rather small. I think the same might have been said, however, of the number of passengers who were directly effected by piracy a hundred or more years ago. For statistical purposes, however, I would like to review some of the more pertinent figures available for 1969 and 1970. In 1969, there were 80 incidents of unlawful seizure of civil aircraft. These involved aircraft of 37 nations around the world and also involved some 5,000

27

passengers representing the citizenship of 83 different nations. In the first three quarters of 1970 there were some 90 incidents of unlawful seizure in this year, of which 24 were aborted. These incidents involved aircraft of 31 different nations; and over 4,300 passengers, whose citizenship represented 89 countries, were placed in danger by these acts of unlawful seizure. This means that in the past one and three quarter years over 9,000 passengers have had their lives jeopardized by the forcible take-over of the control of an aircraft by an individual who is not capable of exercising judgment about the operation of that aircraft.

It is important to note from these figures that while initially many considered this to be a political problem between the United States and Cuba the present involvement of so many States in this problem is a clear indication of its increasing universality. Even though a State's airline may not have been directly affected by unlawful seizure until this time — and there are still some States who are in that fortunate position — it is easy to imagine that the citizens of any nation may be on an aircraft which is the object of an unlawful seizure. Concern for the safety of these passengers should be the concern of all States.

Attempts at legal measures to deal specifically with the problem of unlawful seizure began back in 1962. The United States proposed to have included in the Convention then being drafted on the Legal Status of Aircraft, an article dealing with the crime of unlawful seizure. Included as part of that proposal was a very generally worded provision which would have committed a State who had jurisdiction over a hijacker, either to extradite under existing extradition arrangements or to prosecute the individual if that State's law provided for prosecution of persons responsible for this kind of activity. Unfortuna· ly, the United States proposal came too close to the time when a Diplomatic Conference was being convened for adoption of the Convention on Offences and Certain Other Acts Committed on board Aircraft — the Tokyo Convention. That Convention does not deal with the manner in which a hijacker should be dealt with. Article 11 of the Tokyo Convention is an effort to alleviate the consequences of an unlawful

28

seizure for the passengers, the crew and the aircraft; for it calls for the State where the aircraft lands to permit the passengers, crew and aircraft to continue their journey as soon as practicable.

The Tokyo Convention was signed in 1963 and, by its terms, came into effect 90 days after the date of deposit of the twelfth instrument of ratification. It took *six* years for the twelfth country to ratify the Convention. My own government is hardly blameless for this delay since it was the twelfth State to deposit its instrument of ratification of the Tokyo Convention— in September of 1969. By October, 1970, only 30 countries had ratified the Tokyo Convention, so one may see how slowly States are moving on this one single aspect of the legal framework for dealing with unlawful seizure.

Before I get to the Draft Convention on Unlawful Seizure which I consider to be the present backbone of the legal efforts to deal with this question, I would like to indicate some of the quasi-legal approaches that have been taken through the ICAO forum and the weight that has been given to what has been said at various times. At the 18th Assembly of ICAO, held in 1968 in Buenos Aires, a resolution was adopted which noted that the Tokyo Convention did not provide a complete remedy to the problems created by unlawful seizure. The Council of ICAO was requested by the Assembly to begin a study of other measures to cope with the problem. In December, 1968, the Council passed a resolution condemning acts of unlawful interference with civil aviation. In April, 1969, a resolution adopted by the Council established a Committee on Unlawful Interference to deal with the preventive measures requested by the Assembly. Council debate on the establishment of this Committee was long and arduous, with more heat than light frequently being shed upon the problem. The proposal was to establish the Committee under Article 52 of the Convention on International Civil Aviation which would permit the Committee to take decisions on its own when the Council was not in session. This proposal brought a very vocal response from a minority of the Council; and one would think that the proposal had been the abolition of the Council of ICAO rather than merely a delegation of a certain amount of authority to a Committee made up of members of the Council itself.

Efforts were made from many quarters to dilute the powers which the original proposal had sought to give the Committee. Finally, on April 10, 1969, the Council agreed to adopt a resolution establishing the Committee, under Article 52, but with terms of reference so limited that in essence the Committee was nothing more than a fact-finding group with the power solely to make recommendations to the Council as to preventive measures. It could not effectively deal with any particular situation. This fact was brought home clearly when the United States Government, after the hijacking of a TWA aircraft to Damascus, Syria, sought to make the Committee respond to the extremely serious situation that existed for some time after that incident; but in the United States' view, the Committee was completely unresponsive. The very most that one could get the Committee to do was to cable the Government of Syria to ask for a report on the incident. Of course, that report did not state that two passengers were held for a number of weeks after the plane landed in Damascus; nor did it say anything about the fact that the hijackers, who had partially destroyed the aircraft, were released within days after the incident.

After the sabotage of a Swissair aircraft in February, 1970, and the attempted sabotage of an Austrian Airlines plane at approximately the same time, ICAO convened an Extraordinary Assembly of its Contracting States, to meet in Montreal in June, 1970. Ninety-one countries attended this Assembly which constituted an extraordinary representation of all political elements and geographical areas of the world. Eleven Arab states attended; Israel attended. Nearly all Eastern European countries attended, as well as most Western European countries. Latin American countries were, for the most part, represented, as were most Asian countries with the exception of Communist China. The Assembly produced good work— on paper. It closely examined various technical measures that could be taken to prevent hijacking and the sabotage of aircraft. It also pronounced itself on the policy aspects of unlawful interference. I think you may be interested in some of the language adopted *unanimously* at this Assembly in a Resolution called the Montreal Declaration. It would be my guess that few people have ever heard of this Montreal Declaration; though in fact the delegates from 91 States agreed with the language adopted in this Declaration, which reads as follows:

"THE ASSEMBLY:

CONDEMNS all acts of violence which may be directed against aircraft, aircraft crews and passengers engaged in international civil air transport;

CONDEMNS all acts of violence which may be directed against civil aviation personnel, civil airports and other facilities used by international civil air transport;

URGENTLY

CALLS UPON States not to have recourse, under any circumstances, to acts of violence directed against international civil air transport and airports and other facilities serving such transport;

URGENTLY

CALLS UPON States, pending the coming into force of appropriate international conventions, to take effective measures to deter and prevent such acts and to ensure, in accordance with their national laws, the prosecution of those who commit such acts;

SOLEMNLY

(1) Deplores acts which undermine the confidence placed in air transport by the peoples of the world.

(2) Expresses regret for the loss of life and injury and damage to important economic resources caused by such acts.

(3) Condemns all acts of violence which may be directed against aircraft, crews and passengers engaged in, and against civil aviation personnel, civil airports and other facilities used by, international civil air transport.

(4) Recognizes the urgent need for a consensus among States in order to secure widespread international cooperation in the interests of the safety of international civil air transport.

(5) Requests concerted action on the part of States towards suppressing all acts which jeopardize the safe and orderly development of international civil air transport.

(6) Requests application, as soon as possible, of the decisions and recommendations of this Assembly so as to prevent and deter such acts."

Admittedly, this Resolution is not law. Certainly it is not legally binding on any State, even though the Delegates agreed to it, but it does have a moral force, and that moral force was dealt a severe blow only 22 days after the close of that Assem-

31

bly. It was within that time that an Olympic Airways aircraft was seized in Athens and its passengers held as hostages until the Greek government would agree to release certain terrorists being held in Greek prisons for criminal activities against international airlines. After that agreement was reached, the aircraft departed for another Contracting State of ICAO. The perpetrators of this act, which was directly in defiance and violation of the terms and spirit of that Declaration, went free. The principles of the Declaration agreed to only one month earlier were totally ignored.

The Draft Convention on Unlawful Seizure of Aircraft was, of course, slated for a Diplomatic Conference in The Hague, in December of 1970. The draft had been the object of study by two Sub-Committee meetings and one full Legal Committee meeting of ICAO. In all candor it must be said that the Draft is weak. This weakness was born of the necessity of trying to attract as broad support as possible to a Convention on the subject of unlawful seizure. Over the past two years, each time that a country or group of countries threatened not to accept the Convention if various "strong" provisions should be retained, the draft was further weakened.

I would like to examine, for a moment, some of the weaknesses of this Convention, and generally the efforts of the United States government to have these weaknesses corrected and to provide a much stronger instrument for signature after the Diplomatic Conference at The Hague in December, 1970.

The basic thrust of this Convention is to define the offence of "unlawful seizure" and to provide for a commonly agreed method of dealing with individuals who commit this offence. The first drafts were considered at the Legal Sub-committee meeting in February of 1969. At that meeting, the United States proposed a very simple approach to the problem, namely that unlawful seizure of aircraft be determined to be a common crime and, therefore, subject to extradition in all cases. This approach found little or no support, with many countries taking the position that they could not jeopardize or infringe upon the principle of political asylum even in the case of the crime of hijacking. There was a fall-back, then, to the position where extradition would be no longer mandatory; but where, if a nation did not agree to extradite, then it would be obligated itself to prosecute the individual. Again, questions were raised about the propriety of agreeing, in a treaty, to prosecuting an individual who had committed the offence. Certain of the states raising these particular doubts indicated that their prosecuting authority had to retain discretion as to whether to prosecute, and that they were not able to agree to any Convention making this prosecution mandatory. Again, as a result of these doubts and objections, the terms of the Convention were altered and weakened so that the draft now sent on to the Diplomatic Conference in The Hague in December, 1970, did not actually require prosecution; but rather, if the extradition did not take place, required merely that the case be turned over to the prosecuting authorities of the country refusing extradition for a determination as to whether to prosecute.

It is the United States government's strong belief that, regardless of the motivation of the individual who commits the act, *all* acts of unlawful seizure of aircraft should be punished. In the United States' view, unlawful seizure is an inappropriate method of expression of political demonstration, social hostility, or any other ideological motivation that may cause an individual to commit the act. The United States government fully recognizes that complications can arise from a situation where individuals who are unable, because of their political views, to escape from the nation where they are located in any other fashion, and who therefore decide to hijack an aircraft, are then subject to prosecution. Any such prosecution would, undoubtedly, be undertaken with a great deal of reluctance. Nevertheless, the United States government feels it is not possible to recognize the legitmacy of committing this criminal act, even in the most desperate circumstances; and it is for this reason that the act of hijacking, as such, must be penalised. If extenuating circumstances do exist, they can no doubt be taken into account in assessing the penalty to be applied to the act of hijacking; but the act of hijacking, as such, should not go unpunished.

Another part of this same draft Convention, Article 8, dealt with the question of extradition should that decision to ask

33

for extradition be undertaken by any state having jurisdiction over the hijacker. The U.S. position in relation to the draft Convention was that, in the event of a request for extradition from the State of registration of the aircraft, then that State should have priority, as to extradition. The United States took this position because it believed that the State of registration of the aircraft has the most direct interest in seeing that the criminal act is appropriately dealt with. A proposal to this effect was turned down by the Legal Committee of ICAO, but because of marked changes in circumstances since February, 1970, when the rejection occurred in the ICAO Legal Committee, the United States decided, as its policy for the Diplomatic Conference at The Hague, in December, 1970, once again to seek to strengthen this portion of the Convention.

In sum, the question may be asked whether international law is responding to the social demands being made upon it by the increasing activity of unlawful seizure of aircraft. The short answer is, No! But I hasten to add that international law is not to blame. International law, as the instrument through which the community of nations seeks to express itself in a civilized fashion, is being retarded by the very belated recognition by many countries of the need to deal effectively with the problem of unlawful seizure. I believe that there has been a very serious miscalculation by many countries of the kind of response that is required, through legal instruments, in order to deal effectively with this very serious problem. Any country which feels that it is immune from having this activity used against it, in one fashion or another, is misreading the facts. I do not believe there is a nation on earth that does not have its enemies, real or imagined, and this contageous disease of hijacking may seem attractive to them.

The only firm, and final, solution to the problem is that there should be no safe haven for individuals who commit the act. There must be a recognition, both political and legal, by all nations of the world that their own best interests are served by condemning acts of hijacking by anyone—not only those whose political and social positions they oppose. They must find it in their best interests *today* to agree to effective measure to deal with the problem; to refuse to provide safe haven

34

for hijackers; to remove civil aviation from being a pawn in the political and military activities that go on between the States. Unless and until this recognition gains sufficient universality we are not going to be able to deal effectively with this problem within the framework of international law; and its malignancy could well spread to other vital organs of international commerce, not envisioned by those examining the problem today.

Chapter 3

THE LONDON DRAFT CONVENTION ON ACTS OF
UNLAWFUL INTERFERENCE AGAINST
INTERNATIONAL CIVIL AVIATION

by Gerald F. FitzGerald

"WHEREAS acts of unlawful interference directed against international
civil aviation jeopardize the safety of persons and property, seriously
affect the operation of international air services and undermine the confidence of the peoples of the world in the safety of civil aviation".
These words taken from the Preambular Clause of ICAO Assembly Resolution A17-20, very well sum up the crisis faced
by international civil aviation which, due to acts of international banditry, is no longer able to develop in that "safe and
orderly manner" envisaged in the Preamble to the Convention
on International Civil Aviation. Fortunately, the international
aviation community has not contented itself with anodyne
resolutions condemning these acts. Instead, it has reacted with
practical measures aimed at fighting this new brand of criminal
activity with the weapons of modern technology. It has also
called upon the lawyers of the world to develop a legal framework for the repression of acts of unlawful interference against
international civil aviation.

Even before the scourge of unlawful seizure of aircraft,
commonly called "hijacking", had reached its present epidemic proportions, the International Civil Aviation Organisation had developed the Convention on Offences and Certain
Other Acts Committed on board Aircraft (Tokyo, 1963)
which, in Article 11, contains specific provisions on the unlawful seizure of aircraft. As these provisions were incomplete,
early in 1970, ICAO included more detailed provisions in a
Draft Convention on the Unlawful Seizure of Aircraft, to be

considered at a diplomatic conference at The Hague in December, 1970. Lastly, in view of the upsurge of other acts of interference against international civil aviation, such as attacks against aircraft on the ground and ground installations and the placing of bombs on board aircraft, an Extraordinary Session of the ICAO Assembly, meeting at Montreal in June 1970, instructed the ICAO Legal Committee to prepare a draft convention on acts of unlawful interference against international civil aviation (other than those covered by the Draft Convention on the Unlawful Seizure of Aircraft). The purpose of this note is to examine the history of this subject in ICAO and to discuss briefly the draft convention on Acts of Unlawful Interference which was prepared by the ICAO Legal Committee during its eighteenth session, held in London, between 29 September and 22 October 1970.

The Tokyo Convention on Offences and Certain Other Acts Committed on board Aircraft includes in Article 11 only incomplete provisions concerning the unlawful seizure of aircraft. These were drafted in response to a wave of hijackings in the Caribbean area in the early 1960s and, having been included in the Convention at a late stage of its development, were restricted mainly to providing for the restoration of the aircraft to its lawful commander and the facilitation of the continuance of the journey that had been interrupted by the unlawful seizure. With the sharp upswing in hijackings a few years later and the ever increasing number of incidents of attacks against aircraft and aviation installations during the same period, not to mention the detention of passengers and crew members by certain states of landing, there was great pressure for the preparation of international rules more detailed, and less passive, than those found in the bare-bones provisions of Article 11 of the Tokyo Convention.

Sixteenth Session of the ICAO Assembly (Buenos Aires, September 1968)
Legal Committee, Seventeenth Session (February–March 1970)

The ICAO Assembly, during its Sixteenth Session at Buenos Aires in 1968, decided, in Resolution A16-37, that a convention on the unlawful seizure of aircraft should be developed. After the ICAO Council had taken the necessary action to ensure that the subject was referred to the Legal Committee, a Legal Subcommittee of that body held sessions in February and September-October 1969 and prepared a Draft Convention which was placed before the Legal Committee at its Seventeenth Session, held in February-March 1970. That Session took up as the first substantive item on its agenda the question of the revision of the Warsaw Convention of 1929 as amended by The Hague Protocol of 1955. At the end of the first week of the Session, on 21 February 1970, simultaneous bomb attacks took place on Swiss and Austrian aircraft with tragic results in the case of the Swiss aircraft which was a total loss along with all forty-seven persons on board. These were but the latest in a series of incidents which, by their escalating and cynical savagery, indicated that the unlawful seizure of aircraft was only one phase of the application of violence to international civil aviation.

Seventeenth Session of the ICAO Assembly (Montreal, 16-30 June 1970)

The aviation industry was clearly in a crisis situation and a group of European states soon called for the convening of an extraordinary session of the ICAO Assembly. The purpose of this session was to study the development of adequate security specifications and practices, for application by ICAO states in international civil aviation, aimed at the protection of air passengers, civil aviation personnel and civil aircraft by: (a) preventing criminal acts of any kind that might endanger the safety of air transport and (b) providing for arrangements

38

under which those responsible for criminal actions endangering civil air transport could be brought to justice.

The Assembly met at Montreal from 16 to 30 June 1970 and was attended by ninety-one ICAO Contracting States, one Non-Contracting state and thirteen international organizations. Committee B (Legal Questions) of the Assembly examined the question of the possible preparation of a convention on acts of unlawful interference against international civil aviation. It considered a wide spectrum of ideas on a brainstorming basis since it was here dealing for the first time with acts other than hijacking which was already covered by the Draft Convention of the Unlawful Seizure of Aircraft.

The Assembly adopted Resolution A17-20 which called upon the ICAO Legal Committee to prepare a draft convention on acts of unlawful interference against international civil aviation (other than those already covered by the Draft Convention on the Unlawful Seizure of Aircraft). The Assembly also directed the Legal Committee, in preparing the new draft convention, to take into account the opinions expressed at the Assembly. These opinions were put forward during a protracted debate at the Assembly on the contents of the proposed convention. They are summarized below and it will be seen later to what extent they influenced the Legal Committee in its preparation of the London draft convention.

It was variously suggested to the Assembly that the proposed convention should be concerned with acts of unlawful interference against the safety of aircraft on the ground or in flight, of airports, of installations and all air navigation facilities; acts of violence against aircraft, crew and passengers not covered by the Draft Convention on Ulawful Seizure, and acts of violence against aircraft on the ground, airports and air navigation facilities; violence against aircraft; violence against international civil aviation; acts of unlawful interference against international civil aviation; the repression of terrorism directed at international civil aviation.

Opinions as to the acts constituting the offence fell into the following categories:

(a) *Acts relating to aircraft:* Any of the following acts or omissions, if done without lawful authority, should constitute the offence of violence against aircraft: (i) taking or placing on board an aircraft any device likely to cause damage to the aircraft or to any person or property therein; (ii) causing such a device to be taken or placed on board an aircraft (including mailing a package containing such a device for carriage by air); (iii) activating such a device (including discharging a firearm) or causing such a device to be activated on board an aircraft; (iv) placing or activating any device (including discharging a firearm) or causing any device to be placed or activated in such a position or manner as to be likely to cause damage to an aircraft or any person or property therein; (v) any other act or omission, whether or not of a similar nature to the foregoing, calculated to cause damage to an aircraft or any person or property therein; (vi) attempting or conspiring to commit any of the acts or omissions set out in items (i) to (v) above; (vii) acts of violence against civil aircraft in addition to unlawful seizure; (viii) all offences relating to, or committed on board, aircraft.

(b) *Air navigation:* Offences against air navigation, even where no injury or loss to persons or serious damage to property results.

(c) *Airports, installations and air navigation facilities:* Here the list included: (i) any act of unlawful interference against the safety of aircraft on the ground, of airports, of installations and all air navigation facilities; (ii) acts of unlawful interference against the safety of aircraft on the ground or in flight, of airports, of installations and all air navigation facilities; (iii) acts of violence against aircraft, crew and passengers not covered by the draft convention on unlawful seizure, and acts of violence against aircraft on the ground, airports and air navigation facilities.

(d) *Unlawful interference:* The new convention should, it was variously suggested, refer to (i) "acts of unlawful interference" rather than "acts of violence"; (ii) all acts of unlawful interference against the safety of international civil aviation other than those covered by the convention on the unlawful seizure of aircraft; (iii) acts of sabotage against aircraft and other forms of armed agression against civil aviation.

In the view of many states, the acts covered by the convention should be subject to severe penalties.

Views on jurisdiction varied. Thus, it was stated that the convention should not exclude any jurisdiction exercised in accordance with national law; states should undertake to recognize the principle of legality and establish their penal jurisdiction over offences committed within their territory or on aircraft in flight which land or crash on their territory; among the jurisdictions should be that of the state in which the offender is present when that state does not extradite him.

40

There was recognition by some states and organizations of the international character of the acts concerned and some put forward the view that these acts should be considered as international crimes.

Other provisions suggested for inclusion in the convention concerned arrest of offenders; preliminary inquiry; communication of results of police investigation; prosecution and extradition.

On the question of extradition, one opinion before the Assembly emphasized the need for the non-applicability of the excuse of political motivation; another opinion was that states should undertake to recognize the offences under the convention as entailing extradition to competent contracting states for prosecution; one suggestion was that the question of extradition be dealt with in accordance with extradition treaties and national laws. A further view was that the political motives of the offender will in no circumstances be permitted to influence the subsequent course of his prosecution for the offence. Since the Assembly, news media have reported cases where hijackers whose acts were motivated through political considerations were nevertheless prosecuted by the state of landing which did not extradite them. One state, while denying that there should be any prerogative attaching to a political crime, was in favour of reducing the cases of non-extradition to two: (i) where the death penalty existed in the requesting state; (ii) where the person whose extradition was requested was a national of the requested state. But, in the view of the proponent of this view, the requested state must communicate to ICAO and contracting states the reasons for non-extradition and measures taken for the punishment of the alleged offender.

Further suggestions put before the Assembly were that the convention should include provisions on measures of assistance between states; the furnishing of information by states to one another; assistance to victims and continuance of the voyage as soon as possible; the right to search and examine passengers, baggage, cargo and mail and liability in respect of such search and examination; prohibition against the carriage of arms, munitions and implements of war; renunciation by states of all forms of attacks and sabotage against civil aircraft and their passengers as an instrument of government policy, both in peacetime and wartime, this renunciation to cover: (i) attacks on civil aircraft by the armed forces of the country concerned; (ii) attacks on civil aircraft or their passengers by agents of the government; (iii) sabotage of civil aircraft by armed forces or agents of the government.

Lastly, it was proposed to the Assembly that measures and sanctions be taken against states which failed to comply with their obligations under the convention.

Legal Committee —Eighteenth Session (September-October, 1970)—London Draft Convention

The Draft Convention prepared by the Legal Committee at its Eighteenth Session contains some novel provisions – so novel in fact that the Committee spent the bulk of 26 plenary meetings, five meetings of a special Working Group and five meetings of a Drafting Group in preparing them. For the purposes of this discussion, detailed emphasis will be placed only on the definition of the offences covered by the Draft Convention, the concept of an "aircraft in service", the definition of an "aircraft in flight" and the question of jurisdiction. Since other provisions of the Draft are borrowed, to a great extent from the Draft Convention on the Unlawful Seizure of Aircraft, the definitive text of which was adopted at The Hague conference of December, 1970, only brief descriptive reference will be made to them.

Definition of the offences

At the outset, the Committee decided that the acts constituting the offences should be characterized as being "unlawful". This was because it was necessary to draw a distinction between an unlawful act, on the one hand, and, on the other hand, an act committed under express autority (e.g., the act of an armed guard acting pursuant to authority), an act per-

42

formed with justification (e.g., an act of legitimate self-defence) or a merely negligent act which did not involve criminal negligence.

The element of intention also came in for considerable attention. The question before the Committee was whether, in order for the act to come under the convention, the intention should be directed towards the act itself, towards the consequences of the act or both. The acts and the consequences thereof are described in considerable and varied detail in Article 1 which reads as follows:

A person commits an offence who unlawfully:

(1) intentionally commits an armed attack against the life of a person on board an aircraft in flight; or
(2) intentionally destroys or seriously damages an aircraft in service; or
(3) intentionally damages an aircraft in service with the result of endangering its safety in flight; or
(4) intentionally destroys or damages air navigation facilities with the result of endangering the safety of aircraft in flight; or
(5) intentionally commits an act of interference with the operation of aeronautical communications with the result of endangering the safety of aircraft in flight; or
(6) intentionally places on an aircraft by mail or despatching of cargo or any other means whatsoever a device or substance likely to destroy or seriously damage the aircraft in service of endanger its safety in flight; or
(7) commits any other act or omission with the intention of endangering the safety of aircraft in flight; or
(8) attempts or conspires to commit any of the above acts or omissions; or
(9) is an accomplice of a person who commits or attempts to commit any of the above acts or omissions.

Article 1 is so drafted that the element of unlawfulness applies to all nine of its subparagraphs; that, in the first six subparagraphs, the element of intention applies to the acts therein described and that, in the seventh subparagraph, the element of intention is applied directly to the consequences of an act or omission. A detailed examination of Article 1 follows.

The Committee realized that there were three main categories of unlawful acts to be covered by Article 1: (a) acts performed intentionally; (b) inherently dangerous acts (e.g., placing of a bomb on board an aircraft) from which intention could be inferred, and (c) somewhat equivocal acts (e.g., carriage of radio devices on board aircraft) which might or might not be performed with the intention of endangering the safety of air navigation. Hence, one of the main problems in drafting Article 1 was to specify the kind of acts to be covered by the Article and then to decide in what way the element of intention should be expressed in relation to the various acts.

Before Article 1 of the London Draft is examined in detail, it will be of interest to look at some practical examples of the kind of acts contemplated by that provision:

26 December 1968: Attack against an El Al aircraft at Athens by members of the Popular Front for Liberation of Palestine resulting in the death of an Isreali passenger.

18 February 1969: Attack against an El Al aircraft at Zurich by three members of the Popular Front for Liberation of Palestine resulting in the death of an Israeli pilot.

10 February 1969: Attack against an El Al aircraft at Munich just before take-off resulting in the death of one passenger and the wounding of several people.

21 February 1970: Death of forty-seven persons on board a Swissair Coronado which crashed in Switzerland after an explosion which occurred within fifteen minutes of take-off.

21 February 1970: An Austrian Caravelle carrying mail and passengers to Israel was forced to turn back to Frankfurt shortly after taking off for Vienna when a bomb explosion occurred in a mail compartment. There were no casualties among those on board.

With these unfortunate practical examples in mind, Article 1 may now be considered.

Subparagraph (1) is concerned with an intentional armed attack against the life of a person on board an aircraft in flight. This provision has been placed at the beginning of Article 1 in order to emphasize the importance which the London Draft gives to the protection of human life. The act contemplated involves only an "armed" attack against the physical integrity of the victim. Thus the act will fall within the scope of the convention even if it does not endanger the safety of the aircraft.

Subparagraph (2) refers to the destruction of, or "serious" damage to, an aircraft in service. The term "in service" will be examined later. This subparagraph is intended to cover acts against aircraft on the ground.

44

Subparagraph (3) covers damage to an aircraft, whether in flight or not, with the result of endangering its safety in flight. It overlaps subparagraph (2) in respect of acts committed against aircraft not in flight.

In subparagraph (4), there is a shift to the destruction of, or damage to, air navigation facilities (note that, unlike the case of subparagraph (2), the word "serious" is not used to qualify the word "damage"; nor is there any reference to airports) with the result of endangering the safety of aircraft in flight. The exclusion of airports as a whole from the scope of this provision was made in spite of strong representations of the Delegation of the United Arab Republic that they be included.

Subparagraph (5) refers to the intentional commission of an act of interference with the operation of aeronautical communications with the result of endangering the safety of aircraft in flight. This provision is wide enough to include not only attacks against communications facilities, but also the jamming of such facilities through radio emissions or conceivably, through the unlawful and intentional use of the wrong kind of portable dictating machine on board the aircraft.

In order to take care of incidents, such as those which affected the Swiss and Austrian aircraft on 21 February 1970, where devices are set to detonate when the aircraft reaches a certain altitude, subparagraph (6) categorizes as an offence the intentional placing (which includes the concept of "causing to be placed") on an aircraft by mail or despatching of cargo or by any other means whatsoever a device or substance (the word "substance" being intended to include, items like plastic bombs) "likely to destroy or "seriously" damage the aircraft in service or endanger its safety in flight. The word "likely" is intended to cover the case of placing *inherently* dangerous devices or substances on the aircraft. The expression "*on the aircraft*" covers not only the introduction of the device or substance inside the aircraft, but also the placing of them on the exterior of the aircraft.

The Committee decided, after there had been two tie votes on the question, not to include in Article 1 the principle of prohibition of the carriage of weapons on board an aircraft.

45

The residuary provision in subparagraph (7) states that it is also an offence to commit any other act or omission with the intention of endangering the safety or aircraft in flight. Here, curiously enough, the intention is related to the consequence rather than to the act or omission.

Subparagraphs (8) and (9) borrow the concepts of attempts and complicity from the Draft Convention on the Unlawful Seizure of Aircraft. Subparagraph (8) also includes conspiracy as an offence under the Convention. This idea was strongly opposed by some delegations because according to some national legal systems conspiracy is not an offence.

Aircraft in service

The expression "aircraft in service" is found in a number of places in Article 1 of the Draft Convention. The definition is important since it would specify the circumstances under which acts of the kind contemplated under Article 1 would fall under the Convention. The Committee undertook a detailed consideration of the physical position of the aircraft at the time the acts were committed. Obviously, there would be little difficulty in securing acceptance of the Convention if, by the adoption of a restricted definition, the acts contemplated would come under the Convention only if they were committed against an aircraft in flight (the expression "in flight" is defined below) or were such as to result in endangering the safety of an aircraft or aircraft in flight. But, it may be asked, why should not the definition of the expression "in service" be extended so that the Convention would cover attacks against aircraft in a hangar or when at rest in a parking area? At a major international airport, aircraft with an aggregate value of hundreds of millions of dollars, if not more, may at a given moment be found in hangars and parking areas where they are vulnerable to attack and the international aviation community is interested in the protection of such aircraft. The easy, but not necessarily convincing, answer to the question is that a state where the aircraft are located physically will wish to reserve its jurisdiction over —and not to be bound to extradite — a suspected offender who commits an offence affecting even a foreign aircraft at rest in a hangar or parking area in an airport of that State.

The debate on the definition of the expression "in service" was a difficult one, since apparently no one had ever before attempted to prepare such a definition for penal law purposes and the Committee therefore found itself groping for a description of the physical areas within which the concept of "in service" should apply. Hence, it is not surprising that a number of drafts were prepared before a final solution was reached. These drafts are now considered.

Draft No. 1

"1. For the purposes of this Convention, an aircraft shall be deemed to be 'in service' from the time the aircraft is being prepared at any point of embarkation or loading for a flight until all passengers and crew have disembarked, all baggage and cargo has been unloaded and the aircraft has left the point of disembarkation or unloading."

This draft did not satisfy the Committee since it did not cover all of operations connected with a flight. Therefore, the Committee decided to enlarge the scope of the provision and the Drafting Group prepared the following text:

Draft No. 2

"1. For the purposes of this Convention, an aircraft shall be deemed to be 'in service' from the time when the operational personnel take over the aircraft for the purpose of preparing it for a flight until all passengers and flight personnel have disembarked, all baggage and cargo have been unloaded, the aircraft has been finally parked and the operational personnel have left it. The period during which an aircraft is in service shall include stopovers [outside its State of registry]."

This draft was intended to cover the whole period from the time operational ground personnel taxied or towed the aircraft from the parking area on a large airport to the loading or embarkation area until the time when the aircraft, having been emptied of crew, passengers, baggage and cargo, the operational ground personnel had taxied or towed it to the parking place at the place of arrival and had left it there. It was realized that in a small airport, the parking and loading areas might well coincide. It was also intended that periods while the aircraft was parked at an airport during a stopover, say overnight would not be included within this definition. The Drafting Group was unable at that stage to decide whether the words in square brackets should be included in the definition.

The Committee evidently thought this definition to be too specific and adopted, on third reading, the following provision:

Draft No. 3
"1. For the purposes of this Convention, an aircraft shall be deemed to be 'in service' from the moment of the beginning of its pre-flight handling until final parking at its ultimate destination in its home country."

This makes it clear that from the time the aircraft is taxied or towed from its parking place in the home country until it returns to that country, it is deemed to be "in service". There are some grey areas in the definition. For example, what is meant by "pre-flight handling"? Presumably, under this definition, an aircraft which is parked for extended periods in a foreign country is in service for the purposes of the Convention. The germ of the principle is there and further drafting will give the principle of more precise expression.

A further provision associated with the definition of the expression "in service" states that where any person has unlawfully seized or exercised control of an aircraft in flight, that aircraft shall be deemed to be in service for the entire period of unlawful seizure or exercise of control. This provision brings within the scope of the convention acts committed against an aircraft which, having been hijacked and later landed, is then destroyed by action of the hijackers while it is on the ground. There were some unfortunate examples of this in the Middle East in the Late summer of 1970.

Definition of the expression "in flight"

The definition of the expression "in flight" adopted for the purposes of the Convention is the extensive and artificial one found in Article 5 of the Tokyo Convention on Offences and Certain Other Acts Committed on board Aircraft. For the purposes of the Convention, an aircraft is deemed to be in flight at any time from the moment when its external doors are closed following embarkation until the moment when any such door is opened for disembarkation. Relating this definition back to the expression "with the result of endangering the safety of aircraft in flight" and similar expressions found in Article 1 of the Draft Convention, it is seen that if certain of the acts contemplated in Article 1 are such as to result in endangering the safety of the aircraft at any time while its external doors remain closed after embarkation, these acts fall within the scope of the convention.

Penalties

There was some discussion as to whether the Convention should specify the penalties applicable to the acts contemplated therein. It was finally decided merely to specify, as is done in the Draft Convention on the Unlawful Seizure of Aircraft, that each contracting state undertakes to make the offences in Article 1 punishable by severe penalties.

Civil aircraft

While it was suggested that the protection of military and other state aircraft was also a matter of international concern and that the Convention should apply also to such aircraft, the Committee decided to state in the Convention that it shall not apply to aircraft used in military, customs or police services. In this regard, the Convention follows the formula used in the Chicago Convention on International Civil Aviation and the Tokyo Convention.

Scope of the Convention

The Committee discussed whether the Convention should specifically state that it did not apply to a case where the act performed and the resulting damage were confined to a single state, without any "international element". Here it was suggested that in actual practice no state whose interests were not directly affected by an incident was likely to claim jurisdiction or request extradition. Accordingly, it was decided that it was unnecessary to include in the Convention a statement concerning the "international element".

Jurisdiction

The London Draft provides that each Contracting State shall take such measures as may be necessary to establish its jurisdiction over the offences in Article 1 in the following cases: (a) when any such offence has been committed in the territory of that State; (b) when any such offence has been committed on board an aircraft registered in that State or against such an aircraft; and (c) when the effect of any such offence has occurred in the territory of that State.

To take care of the case of leased aircraft it is provided that each Contracting State [shall] [may] — the Committee has not reached a decision on the options in square brackets — take the necessary measures to establish its jurisdiction over the offences in Article 1 when such offences are committed on board an aircraft operated by a carrier who has his head office in that State, even though the aircraft may not be owned by the carrier.

The Convention does not exclude any criminal jurisdiction exercised in accordance with national law.

Procedures for arrest, detention and preliminary enquiry

Like the Tokyo Convention and the Draft Convention on the Unlawful Seizure of Aircraft, the London Draft provides that, upon being satisfied that the circumstances so warrant, any Contracting State in the territory of which the alleged offender is present, shall take him into custody or take other measures to ensure his presence. The custody and other measures shall be as provided in the law of that State, but may only be continued for such time as is reasonably necessary to enable any criminal or extradition proceedings to be instituted. Having taken these measures, the State is bound immediately to make a preliminary enquiry into the facts. Any person in custody in pursuance of the above provisions shall be assisted in communicating immediately with the nearest appropriate representative of the State of which he is a national. The State taking custody shall immediately notify the State of registration of the aircraft and the State of nationality of the detained person and, if it considers it advisable, any other interested States of the fact that such person is in custody and of the circumstances which warrant his detention. The State which makes the preliminary enquiry already mentioned must promptly report its finding to the State of registration of the aircraft and the State of nationality of the detained person and indicate whether it intends to exercise jurisdiction.

Prosecution

The London Draft next provides, as in the case of the Draft Convention on the Unlawful Seizure of Aircraft, that the Contracting State which has taken the above described measures, including detention of the alleged offender, shall, if it does not extradite the alleged offender, be obliged to submit the case to its competent authorities for their decision whether to prosecute him. These authorities must take their decision in the same manner as in the case of other offences.

Extradition

Article 8 of the London Draft provides, like the Draft Convention on the Unlawful Seizure of Aircraft, that the offence shall be deemed to be included as an extraditable offence in any extradition treaty existing or to be concluded between Contracting States; that the offence shall be recognized as an extraditable offence as between States which do not require an extradition treaty for purposes of extradition; and that, for the purpose of extradition, the offence shall be deemed to have been committed also in the State of registration of the aircraft or of the State in which the aircraft lands with the offender on board. The Committee decided not to entertain a proposal that "the acts enumerated in Article 1 shall not be considered as political crimes for the purpose of extradition". In view of this decision, the Committee noted, but took no decision on, a Brazilian proposal to the effect that: "The Committee should discuss the principle that the offences enumerated in Article 1 shall not be considered as political crimes for the purposes of this Convention and forward its views to the Diplomatic Conference."

Similarly, the Committee noted, but took no decision on a Netherlands proposal the effect of which was to provide that: "The Contracting States which make extradition conditional on the existence of a treaty undertake to conclude treaties with all other Contracting States in order to make the offence extraditable, if no extradition treaty exists between them."

Joint or international registration of aircraft

Borrowing from Article 5 of the Draft Convention on the Unlawful Seizure of Aircraft, the London Draft provides that the Contracting States which establish joint air transport operating organizations or international operating agencies, which operate aircraft which are subject to joint or international registration shall, by appropriate means, designate for each aircraft the State among them which shall exercise the jurisdiction and have the attributes of the State of registration for the purposes of the Convention and shall give notice thereof to ICAO which shall communicate the notice to all States parties to the Convention.

Refusal of a state to admit a person

The Committee discussed, but decided only to note, a proposal that the Draft Convention should include the provisions of Article 14 of the Tokyo Convention relating to the case of a person whom the state of landing refuses to admit and who cannot, or does not desire, to continue his journey.

Continuance of journey

In line with ICAO Seventeenth Assembly Resolutions A17-5 (Measures recommended for adoption to alleviate the consequences of an unlawful seizure) and A17-8 (Return of unlawfully seized aircraft, their crews, passengers and cargoes) and following the precedents found in Article 11, paragraph 2 of the Tokyo Convention and Article 9 of the Draft Convention on the Unlawful Seizure of Aircraft, the London Draft provides that when, due to the commission of an offence in Article 1, a flight has been delayed or interrupted, the Contracting States in whose territory the aircraft or passengers or crew are located: (a) shall take all appropriate measures to restore control of the aircraft to its lawful commander or to preserve his control of the aircraft; (b) shall permit the passengers and crew to continue their journey as soon as practicable, and (c) shall return the aircraft and its cargo to the persons lawfully entitled to possession.

Assistance in legal proceedings and information on investigation

Article 11, as in the case of the Draft Convention on the Unlawful Seizure of Aircraft, provides for mutual assistance between states, in accordance with applicable law, in connection with proceedings brought in respect of an offence, and Article 12, like the Draft Convention on the Unlawful Seizure of Aircraft, is concerned with the furnishing of information by one State to another with regard to an offence committed or about to be committed.

53

One proposal placed before the Committee and included in the London Draft in square brackets (in order to indicate that the Committee did not adopt the text) is that, upon request of the ICAO Council, each Contracting State shall report to ICAO as rapidly as possible any relevant information in its possession concerning: (a) the circumstances of any offence in Article 1; (b) the action taken to enable the aircraft, passengers and crew to continue their journey, and (c) the measures taken in relation to the alleged offender, and, in particular, the result of any extradition proceedings or other legal proceedings.

Conclusion

The London Draft Convention on Acts of Unlawful Interference against International Civil Aviation is not a perfect instrument. Nevertheless it will serve as a useful basis for further study and when adopted in final form by a Diplomatic Confenrence in 1971 will mark an important contribution by the lawyers of the aviation community to overcoming one of the greatest crises ever faced by any mode of transportation. The challenge is great. But one may be sure that the collective legal wisdom marshalled by ICAO contracting states will be equal to the task of meeting this challenge.

COMMENT

Hijacking. The Limitations of the International Treaty Approach

by Michel Pourcelet

On December 12th, 1969, the General Assembly of the United Nations adopted a text of Resolution concerning forcible diversion of civil aircraft in flight. This Resolution called upon states to take every appropriate measure to ensure that their respective national legislations provide an adequate framework for effective legal measures against all kinds of acts of unlawful interference with, seizure of, or other wrongful exercise of control, by force or threat thereof, over civil aircraft in flight. The Resolution also invited states to ratify or accede to the Convention on Offences and Certain Other Acts Committed on Board Aircraft, signed in Tokyo in 1963.

According to Professor Evans, hijacking is a kind of Russian roulette; and one wonders whether such a dangerous game can be controlled or abolished by the present international legislations.

The increase in the number of hijackings in 1969 (70% are apparently committed for political reasons) has led some states to ratify the Tokyo Convention which came into force between the contracting states on December 4, 1969.

In this respect, one may say that from a general point of view, it is quite unbelievable that such a convention, which required only twelve ratifications to come into legal effect, did not come into force until more that six years after its first adoption at the Tokyo diplomatic conference. At this stage, one can wonder about the value given to an international treaty by the various governments which seemed, at the time of drafting, quite in agreement with its content. Furthermore, it is rather sad that only a crisis affecting deeply the national interest of a country seems to be able to incite a government to fulfil its international obligations.

The Tokyo Convention deals with offences and acts committed on board aircraft; and article 11 of the Convention concerns the unlawful seizure of aircraft, the powers and duties of States being established by articles 13 and 14. It is not my purpose to deal at length with the various dispositions contained in the Convention, since that has been done in a very effective manner in the previous papers.

I would merely say that the international treaty is now outdated and inaccurate to solve the problems that now confront the whole world. However, (save for the most recent text adopted at The Hague in December. 1970) the Tokyo Convention is the only multilateral treaty dealing partly with hijackings. It is unfortunate that it does not state a strict international procedure requiring prosecution of the offender, but, rather, establishes the necessary steps to be taken by the authorities in case of unlawful seizure of aircraft.

Upon reading the new draft convention prepared by the ICAO Legal Committee in order to remedy this inadequate legislation, it does not seem that all the problems have been confronted.

First, concerning the scope of application of the Convention text submitted to the diplomatic conference of The Hague in December, 1970, the rule enacted in article 2 (3) seems to be too restrictive when it states that the Convention shall apply only if the place of take off or the place of landing of the aircraft on board which the offence is committed, is situated outside the territory of the state of registration of that aircraft. The Convention should cover not only international acts of hijacking but also domestic acts,—that is to say, acts occurring on a flight which began and ended on the territory of the state of registration of the aircraft concerned,—in order to internationalise the offence. The restrictive drafting of article 2 (3) is somehow illogical since the Convention applies to seizure committed on a domestic flight if the flight is performed by an aircraft in another state. Since domestic flights performed by foreign carriers fall within the scope of the Convention, it is hard to understand that a domestic flight performed by an aircraft registered in the overflown state could be exempted.

The criticisms addressed to the limited scope of article 2 (3) would not be necessary if the countries had adopted or would adopt laws relating to acts of unlawful seizure, incorporating in the national legislation the dispositions of the international Convention.

On reading the actual legislations in force, one sees clearly the differences between the various laws, — for example, in regard to the question of penalties.

Consequently, I strongly believe that this matter should have been paid more attention and article 2 (3) reconsidered before or during the diplomatic conference.

As a second point, some other problems seem to arise from the actual draft Convention.

Normally, the state of registration of the aircraft should be, in all cases, competent to establish its jurisdiction over the offence; and the contracting states, including the state where the aircraft lands, should, on request, extradite the perpetrators of the offence of unlawful seizure. But we know already that unlawful seizure of aircraft is often a political act and that a state will not prosecute the offender, being the national of foreign country, who has asked for political asylum.

Consequently, the internationalisation of the Convention,—by having its dispositions applied in the case of domestic or international flights, or by recognizing the offence as an international crime —would not be enough to secure prosecution of the offender.

Now if we turn to the problem which was raised in the ICAO Legal Committee concerning aircraft registered in a state other than the state of nationality of the operator, it is quite unfortunate that the Legal Committee did not state a disposition in the draft convention on this matter, apparently leaving it to be examined at the diplomatic conference.

Aircraft leasing is nowadays a widespread practice; and during the meetings of the Legal Committee, the view was expressed that the state of which the operator was a national might have a greater interest in securing the prosecution of the alleged offender than the state of registration. But what would happen if the state of which the operator is a national is not a contracting party to the Convention? The extradition could be refused, since article 8 (2) would not apply. And even if the Convention does not exclude any criminal jurisdiction exercised in accordance with national laws, the national law should be in existence.

Therefore, it would be opportune, in case of aircraft leasing, to maintain the jurisdiction over the offence of the state of registration or of the state in which the aircraft lands.

My general feeling about the Convention is that, once again, the draft as submitted at The Hague in December, 1970, does not go far enough. In order to protect a certain legal chauvinism well established among the countries, the Convention did not impose penalties. Each contracting state undertakes to make the offence punishable by severe penalties, according to article 3. What does it mean? According to the laws relating specifically to the acts of unlawful seizure of aircraft, the penalties vary from three years of imprisonment, to the death penalty. Consequently the same crime will not be treated in the same way, and the future hijackers should consider carefully, before committing the offence, their final destination; and they should then choose the plane which will take them there. In this sense, hijacking is a kind of Russian roulette.

In terms of conclusion, I would like to say that I believe that hijacking is perhaps more a technical problem than a legal one. Hijacking should be prevented on the ground and in the air. Technicians, airport authorities, and airline companies should provide, if not a definitive solution, at least a means to slow down the almost day to day practice.

Chapter 4

THE INTERNATIONAL LAW OF AERIAL PIRACY
NEW PROPOSALS FOR THE NEW DIMENSION

by John B. Rhinelander*

I think we should be under no illusions as to the threat that civil aviation—domestic and international—faces today; and here I should advise you, right at the outset, concerning the contemporary mood in Washington as to hijacking of aircraft. There is, in fact, complete agreement on the need to take effective, prompt and comprehensive action to eliminate what President Nixon has called an "international menace."

Hijacking, from the point of view of the United States, became a serious problem in 1961. At that time, however, many governments viewed hijacking primarily as a U.S.-Cuban matter, not one affecting the international community generally. The Tokyo Convention (Convention on Offences and Certain Other Acts Committed on Board Aircraft), signed in 1963, contains one important article relating to hijacking, but does not deal with the punishment of hijackers. As the threat increased and became recognized by governments generally, initiatives by the United States and other countries seeking to deal with the problem of punishing hijackers on a multilateral basis have gradually received broader acceptance. The draft Convention on Hijacking (approved by the 17th Session of the Legal Committee of ICAO in March 1970)[1] and the draft Convention on Sabotage and Other Attacks on Aircraft (ap-

* The views expressed in this paper are the author's and do not necessarily represent the position of the Department of State.

[1] The draft Convention was formally adopted at the International Conference on Air Law at The Hague on December 16, 1970, (with significant amendments, however, to the original draft text).

proved by the specially-convened 18th Session of the Legal Committee) are the products of an increased awareness in the past few years that States must take actions to punish hijackers and deny them safe havens.

This year governments have been confronted with the fact that threats to aviation are more menacing than ever before. International lawyers, and particularly lawyers in governments around the world, are seeking more effective means to bring law and evolving policy into line — means which can be implemented promptly.

The United States government believes that one of the most effective deterrents to hijacking and other violent acts against aircraft would be acknowledgment by all States that perpetrators are to be subject to punishment wherever they may be.[2] This requires broadened national legislation and agreement among all States to extradite offenders or prosecute them.

Events in the past year are demonstrative evidence that the present threat to civil aviation as a whole is a real and immediate one. A few facts and examples will suffice.

First, the hijacking threat is universal. It is not confined to hijack-prone flights or regions where special precautionary measures could be taken. In 1970 alone hijackers have struck at aircraft registered in the United States, Great Britain, Switzerland, Japan, Brazil, Costa Rica, Israel, Czechoslovakia, Roumania, the Soviet Union, and other States.

Again, the motives of hijackers vary. Some are common criminals, others are psychopaths or alcoholics. Recently, organized political revolutionaries have callously threatened the lives of hundreds of innocent passengers in an attempt to force governments to acquiesce to their blackmail demands.

The weapons hijackers use vary. While a knife or pistol was common in the early 1960s, we now see shotguns and automatic weapons, and, more ominously, hand grenades and other explosives.

Hijackers have demonstrated that they are willing to use

[2] The Convention on Hijacking, as adopted at The Hague in December, 1970, provides for universal jurisdiction in Article 4, paragraph 2.

60

their weapons even at the expense of their own lives. Pilots have been killed or wounded while at the controls; a stewardess was recently killed; and one hijacker actually released a hand grenade which fortunately proved to be a dud.

The fact that most hijackings of U.S.-registered aircraft have been to Cuba, and the hijacked aircraft, passengers and crew have returned to the United States within a relatively short period of time, cannot obscure two basic points. First, every hijacking endangers the passengers and crew members aboard; and second, we have seen hijackings for international blackmail purposes spread from the Middle East to Cuba. A recent case, concerning a Costa Rican aircraft hijacked in October, 1970, involved seven armed extremists who threatened to kill four American citizens unless Costa Rica agreed to the release of four prisoners.

In addition to hijacking, the threat of sabotage of aircraft in flight and attacks against aircraft on the ground is before us. In February, 1970, an Austrian aircraft was seriously damaged and a Swiss aircraft destroyed while in flight. The threat of sabotage could prove to be much more serious to civil aviation than hijacking.

The primary concern in responding to the new dimension of the hijacking threat is, of course, to ensure the safety and well-being of passengers and crew to the greatest extent possible. All decisions which President Nixon has taken to date, and which the United States government will take in the future, are based on this primary objective.

Any response, it cannot be doubted, involves risks and costs—political, legal and economic—and may involve risks to passengers and crew in cases where the failure to act would create graver risks. All decisions governments take—declaratory of general policy, and in a particular case—must be measured against *the risks and costs of the failure of governments or the aviation community generally to act at all or only halfheartedly.*

Recent efforts of governments to curb hijacking have been directed toward security measures at airports and on board aircraft. Such measures were the subject of intense examination of the Extraordinary Seventeenth ICAO Assembly, which met in Montreal in June, 1970. Among the steps that have been inaugurated are examination of passengers by use of electronic and other surveillance devices; physical searches of men and women, and their luggage (including persons travelling under diplomatic passports); and the use of various kinds of profiles on potential hijackers. While costly, time-consuming, inconvenient and even annoying, these measures are clearly among the most important steps which can be taken. Other security measures have been taken around the perimeters of airports, on the field, and inside buildings. On board aircraft procedures have been developed to warn crew members of possible hijacking attempts. Some governments, including the United States, have decided to place specially-trained guards on board commercial airlines.

In recognizing the importance of these security measures as deterrents to hijacking, one must, nonetheless, take cognizance of their limits. No response or series of responses of this type by governments or the aviation community can put a complete and final stop to hijackings or acts of sabotage and other attacks. Thus, it is of primary importance that governments agree to prosecute all hijackers, and that they agree to act in concert to see that such a principle is observed by all States. If some States provide asylum from prosecution for hijacking, the combined efforts of other States to deter hijacking by ensuring that hijackers are prosecuted will to a certain extent by undercut.

One of the seven points which President Nixon announced on September 11, 1970, to deal with the hijacking problem was to seek international agreement that joint action—specifically the suspension of air services—is an appropriate step against States refusing to extradite or punish hijackers involved in international blackmail (Department of State Bulletin, September 28, 1970, p. 341).

On September 18, 1970 the U.S. Secretary of Transportation, John A. Volpe, formally proposed that the ICAO Council adopt a two-fold resolution calling for joint suspension of air services in the international blackmail type of hijacking cases where the offenders are not extradited or prosecuted, and directing the ICAO Legal Committee to prepare a Convention to formalize procedures for consultation and joint action by States (Department of State Bulletin, October 19, 1970, p. 449). At the same time, Canada proposed a bilateral approach which would supplement the U.S. multilateral proposal.

On October 1, 1970, the Council of ICAO adopted an amended version of the resolution proposed by the United States. The vote was 14 in favor, 3 against and 10 abstentions. (The original and final versions of the resolution are printed in the Department of State Bulletin, October 19, 1970, p. 453). The United States was heartened by the action of the ICAO Council and particularly by the fact that all the major ICAO Council States with one exception voted in favor of the resolution. The Canadian bilateral approach was also approved by the Council at the same session.

On October 9, 1970, the United States Delegation to the ICAO Legal Committee, which was then meeting in London, distributed as a working document a draft Convention on Sanctions.[3] The Legal Committee had earlier agreed to extend its session for an extra ten days to begin the difficult job of reviewing and analyzing the U.S. and Canadian proposals which had been adopted by the Council. The report of the Legal Commmittee recommended to the Council that a Legal Subcommittee be established and convened, if practicable, as early as November or December of 1970, in The Hague, to continue work on the U.S. and Canadian proposals.[4]

The basic thrust of the draft Convention on Sanctions proposed by the United States is quite simple. It rests on the following main premises. States are obligated to permit passengers and crew of a hijacked aircraft to continue on their journey as soon as practicable and to restore the aircraft to persons lawfully entitled to possession. Again, to ensure the safety and security of international civil air transport, States should extradite or prosecute all hijackers, and especially those involved in international blackmail cases, and persons causing damage to an aircraft or death or physical injury to passengers or crew.

[3] LC/WD 776. Reprinted as Appendix 8, *infra.*
[4] The Subcommittee was finally scheduled to meet from April 14 to 27, 1971, in Montreal.

The draft Sanctions Convention, therefore, provides that if a State detains an aircraft, its passengers or crew for blackmail purposes, or if a State fails to extradite or prosecute hijackers involved in international blackmail or other persons causing damage to an aircraft or death or physical injury to persons on board, other States may take joint action against such State, including the suspension of all air services to and from it. The Convention provides the necessary procedural and decision-making framework for this concerted State action.

We are immediately confronted with at least three major questions when we consider a convention in which States might suspend air services in certain kinds of cases.

First, what is the basis under international law for sanctions?

Second, how would decisions be made under the convention, and to what extent would they be binding on States?

Third, would sanctions ever be used?

Legal Basis for Convention on Sanctions

The Convention on Sanctions proposed by the U.S. government is based on principles set forth in three multilateral conventions — one in force and two still in draft form.[5]

The first set of principles are those in Article 11 of the Tokyo Convention of 1963. The basic rule in that Article is that a State in which a hijacked aircraft lands is required to permit passengers and crew to continue on their journey as soon as practicable, and to return the aircraft to the persons lawfully entitled to possession. The U.S. government believes that this rule — analogous to rules applicable to mariners in distress, which are reflected in customary international law — reflects general principles of international air law binding on all States.

The second set of principles which lay the foundation for the draft Convention on Sanctions are found in Articles 6, 7

[5] The Convention on Hijacking, as originally drafted, was strengthened in several respects in the text as finally adopted at The Hague in December, 1970.

64

and 8 of the draft Convention on Hijacking approved by the Legal Committee of ICAO at its 17th Session. The U.S. government put forward various suggestions, at the diplomatic conference held at The Hague in December, 1970, designed to strengthen these Articles. The standards for State actions which will eventually be incorporated in the Sanctions Convention will be those adopted by the diplomatic conference for the Convention on Hijacking, held at The Hague in December, 1970. In the original draft Convention, Articles 6, 7 and 8 obligated a State in which a hijacked aircraft had landed to take a hijacker into custody, and thereafter to extradite him or refer the case to competent authorities for their decision on whether to prosecute him. These Articles in the original draft Convention, especially insofar as they dealt with the obligation to prosecute persons causing harm to aliens, reflected certain general principles of international law dealing with state responsibility. Equally important, it is the considered judgment of the United States that the failure to take into custody and prosecute all hijackers—whatever the motivation in a particular case—encourages other hijackings and increases the threat to civil aviation. The U.S. government regards it as appropriate for States to protect the safety of civil aviation generally by taking action against States, whether or not parties to the Convention on Hijacking, which fail to take into custody, and extradite or prosecute, hijackers. Anything less would be an admission that States cannot, or should not, act in concert to ensure the safety and security of civil aviation.

The third set of principles which form the basis for the draft Convention on Sanctions are to be found in Articles 6, 7 and 8 of the draft Convention on Sabotage and Other Attacks on Aircraft (referred to, technically, by the Legal Committee of ICAO as the Convention on Acts of Unlawful Interference Against International Civil Aviation). This Convention was prepared by the Legal Committee during its London session which ended on October 22, 1970. It will probably be considered at a diplomatic conference in the summer of 1971.[6]

[6] A diplomatic conference has been scheduled for September 8-23, 1971.

This Convention contains obligations in Articles 6, 7 and 8 identical to those of the original draft Convention on Hijacking. The principal difference between the two Conventions is in the nature of the unlawful acts covered by each one, defined in Article 1. The Convention on Hijacking is limited to acts of unlawful seizure of aircraft, and attempts; while the Convention on Sabotage and Other Attacks on Aircraft includes armed attacks against persons on board aircraft, any intentional acts to destroy or seriously damage air navigation facilities or interfere with the operation of aeronautical communications having the result of endangering the safety of aircraft in flight. Critical to the relationship of this Convention to the Convention on Sanctions is the belief that the failure to punish persons who in fact cause damage to aircraft in flight or death or physical injury to passengers or crew represents a threat to civil aviation of equal magnitude to hijackings for blackmail purposes.

Machinery of Draft Convention on Sanctions

A further major question as to the draft Convention on Sanctions relates to the decision-making process and the cognate issue of the binding nature of any decision taken.

The proposed draft Convention on Sanctions rests on a two-step procedure. As the first step, any State directly affected by a hijacking or detention of aircraft for blackmail purposes or any unlawful interference with an aircraft causing damage to the plane, or death or physical injury to passengers or crew, may invoke the appropriate machinery of Article 2 or Article 3 for the purpose of determining default by a State with respect to the obligations of Article 11 of the Tokyo Convention of 1963; of Articles 6, 7 and 8 of the draft Convention on Hijacking; or of Articles 6, 7 and 8 of the draft Convention on Sabotage and Other Attacks on Aircraft. As the second step, if a State is found to be in default—for example, if it does not extradite or prosecute a hijacker involved in an international blackmail case—then States can determine, pursuant to Article 4 of the draft Convention on Sanctions, what joint action, if any, to take. The Convention specifically provides that joint action may include the suspension by States providing air services of authority to operate international civil air service directly or indirectly to and from the State determined to be in default.

The basic framework of the draft Convention on Sanctions permits States, whether or not parties to the Convention, to participate in the decision-making process and to decide on action to be taken. It is framed so that joint action can be applied, pursuant to the Convention, against a State even though it is not a party. Finally, it provides that a decision to impose sanctions, taken by a majority of the States entitled to participate and vote in the consultations on joint action contemplated by the Convention, is binding on all States parties to the Convention which are entitled to participate and vote in the consultations, whether or not actually participating and voting. Such a decision is recommendatory with respect to all non-contracting States.

As might be imagined, this draft was the subject of intense debate in London at the 18th Session of the Legal Committee; even though the time available for consideration was short, due to the need to complete the work on the draft Convention on Sabotage and Other Attacks on Aircraft. Many delegates did not have instructions from their governments on the draft Convention on Sanctions, but this did not stop them from raising questions and engaging in useful discussions.

The report of the Legal Committee summarized the points on which there appeared to be general agreement, and also the principal policy and legal issues which will have to be reviewed. One may expect this to speed the process of consideration by governments so that their representatives can be fully instructed when the Legal Subcommittee convenes.

One of the basic points raised by the delegates in London was the compatibility of the draft Convention on Sanctions with the Chicago Convention of 1944. The U.S. government does not believe, following on the debate at the 18th Session, that any serious question should remain in regard to this issue. The Preamble of the Chicago Convention, and also Articles 4, 25 and 44(a) and (b), can lead to no other conclusion than that jointly-taken steps, designed to provide for the safe and orderly development of international air transport services, are fully consistent with the objectives of the draft Convention on Sanctions.

While the issue was not discussed in detail, some delegates queried whether the draft Convention on Sanctions could provide for joint action against a State not a contracting party, and perhaps not a party to the three underlying Conventions. They cited Articles 34 through 36 of the Vienna Convention on the Law of Treaties. The U.S. government believes that the scope and application of the draft Convention is justified on the basis of the fundamental objective to provide safe and secure international civil air tranportation and the general principles arising out of the three underlying Conventions, as earlier referred to.

Generally, delegates favored the two-step procedure proposed by the U.S. government—the first to determine default, and the second to determine what joint action to take. Delegates also generally agreed on the need to provide for emergency procedures, as proposed in Article 2; and non-emergency procedures for Article 3 cases.

The draft Convention provides that determination of default in regard to detention by a State of hijacked passengers or crew or the aircraft (Article 2 cases) shall be made by certain States. Determination of default in regard to failure by a State to extradite or prosecute hijackers involved in international blackmail, or persons who unlawfully interfere with an aircraft, causing damage to it or death or physical injury to passengers or crew members (Article 3 cases), would be made by a five-man tribunal. Views varied at the Legal Committee as to whether this machinery for determinations of default, or a tribunal approach for both Article 2 and 3 cases, should be preferred.

The need to define in precise legal terms the phrase "international blackmail" was stressed by almost all delegates. Some delegates, however, suggested that this limitation be dropped and that sanctions should be imposed in *all* hijacking and unlawful interference cases if a State fails to extradite or prosecute the offender. Others agreed with the approach in the draft Convention which focuses on the particularly heinous cases.

The draft Convention establishes different rôles for States, depending on their relationship to a particular case. States affected in a case are defined, either as "Interested States" or "Air Service States", in Article 1. The rights and obligations of the two categories of States are subjects certain to merit close attention by the Legal Subcommittee which has been established to consider the Convention on Sanctions. Critical questions, concerning the right to participate and vote in consultations to determine default and the nature of joint action to be taken, will have to be answered. These issues received only brief attention at the 18th Session.

Finally, delegates to the Legal Committee commented on the fact that States not parties to the Convention would be entitled to participate in determinations of default and decisions to impose sanctions. The most important question of all—the binding quality of a decision and whether it should be made by mere majority vote—was raised but not fully explored, due to a lack of time.

All of these issues and others, including the suggestion that the draft Convention on Sanctions should perhaps be in the form of an amendment to the Chicago Convention of 1944, will be examined in depth when the Legal Subcommittee meets.

Will Sanctions Ever be Used?

The third question, raised earlier, which must be faced at the highest levels of governments is whether sanctions will ever be used.

A policy to support the principle of sanctions is, of course, quite different from taking a decision to implement joint action in a given case. The question whether a sanction, such as suspension of air services, would ever be used, involves sensitive and difficult political, economic and legal considerations for every State. There would be, without question, a reluctance on the part of many States to impose such a drastic remedy. On the other hand, there is general acceptance of the fact that sanctions, if they are to be effective at all, must be undertaken in concerted action by all or almost all States involved. And there is the ominous possibility that if States fail to act together in a particularly reprehensible case, the general public, pilots, airline or transport associations may feel a need to act on their own, independently of government policies.

The United States has proposed formalising the structure for the taking of sanctions, with a number of objectives in mind. Not only does the U.S. government see a Convention on Sanctions as a deterrent to hijacking, in that its very existence lends strength to the principle that States must prosecute hijackers. Such a Convention on Sanctions will also provide readily-available machinery, if necessary in an exceptionally grave case, to ensure observance of the fundamental principles of the Tokyo Convention of 1963, and of the Convention on Hijacking and the Convention on Sabotage and Other Attacks on Aircraft. The U.S. government believes it is for these reasons that suspension of air services has for so long been advocated by the international pilots association, IFALPA. It is to be noted that this IFALPA proposal was strongly endorsed by IATA and IFTU Observers at the 18th Session of the Legal Committee.

In conclusion, one must take note of the swift pace of events in recent times, both in terms of the heightened threat, which has added a new dimension to the hijacking problem, and in terms also of attempts to cope with that heightened threat. Governments, and particularly their lawyers dealing with aviation matters, have reacted with much greater speed and have been quick to formulate policies as the crisis aviation faced has become clearer.

One must especially consider the resulting international calendar which has imposed extraordinarily heavy demands on government lawyers as a result of a continuing series of conferences on aviation matters.

In order to deal adequately with the complex nature of unresolved aviation problems, a sixteen-day diplomatic conference met at The Hague in December, 1970, to adopt a Convention on Hijacking. Thereafter, a Legal Subcommittee was to be at work on the Sanctions issue. In February, 1971, a month-long diplomatic conference was slated to meet in Guatemala City to consider revision of the Warsaw Convention. The Summer of 1971 should see both the 18th ICAO Assembly meeting for a month in Vienna; and also a diplomatic conference on the Convention on Sabotage and Other Attacks on Aircraft.

All in all, aviation problems will continue to demand enormous expenditures of time and effort. But the severity of the problems demands nothing less.

Chapter 5

SECURING THE ENFORCEMENT OF INTERNATIONAL
LEGAL OBLIGATIONS RELATING TO UNLAWFUL
INTERFERENCE WITH INTERNATIONAL CIVIL
AVIATION; CANADIAN INITIATIVES

by P.A. Bissonnette and L.S. Clark

The international community has been increasingly concerned
with the need to develop an effective international legal framework to prevent and deter acts of unlawful interference against
civil aviation. Since 1961 when the first aircraft hijacking to be
prominently reported by the mass communications media
took place, there has been a steady growth in the frequency
and seriousness of such acts. By the end of the third quarter of
1971, we had witnessed not only seizure of control of civil
aircraft at gun and knife point, machine-gunning of commercial airliners on the ground and sabotage of international pas-
senger-carrying planes in flight, but also the holding of private
civilian men, women and children air travellers as hostages for
blackmail purposes and the deliberate destruction by explosive
devices of millions of dollars worth of jetliners.

ICAO Conventions

The first international air law instrument which addressed
itself to the question of unlawful acts against civil aviation was
the Convention on Offences and Certain Other Acts Committed on Board Aircraft. The ICAO Legal Committee Draft,
on which the final text was based, had taken several years to
elaborate and it was eventually signed on September 14th,
1963 in Tokyo. It came into force—after the required deposit

72

of the twelfth instrument of ratification — on December 4th, 1969. Canada ratified the Convention on November 7, 1969 and it came into force for Canada on February 5, 1970, that is, after the Convention as a whole had come into force. The major provisions of the Convention with respect to unlawful interference with civil aviation concern jurisdiction; powers of the aircraft commander; unlawful seizure; and powers and duties of States.

As a result of the large number of hijackings which took place in the latter part of the 1960s, the Sixteenth ICAO Assembly meeting in Buenos Aires in September 1968, adopted Resolution A16-37 on Unlawful Seizure of Civil Aircraft. This Resolution noted that Article 11 of the Tokyo Convention provides certain, but not complete, remedies for the situation envisaged and, inter alia, requested the ICAO Council:

"At the earliest possible date, to institute a study of other measures to cope with the problem of unlawful seizure."

In conformity with this request, the ICAO Council instructed the Chairman of the Legal Committee to establish a Special Subcommittee on Unlawful Seizure of Aircraft. The Sub-Committee held two meetings in February and September-October 1969 during the course of which it completed a Draft Convention on Unlawful Seizure of Aircraft. The Seventeenth Session of the Legal Committee considered this draft in March 1970 and, at the conclusion of the session, approved a revised draft text which it viewed as being ready for reference to a Diplomatic Conference. The Conference is scheduled to take place at The Hague, December 1-16, 1970.

Key articles in the present Draft deal with definition and establishment of the offence; jurisdiction; prosecution and punishment of offenders; and extradition.

Following the explosions on board regularly scheduled flights of Swissair and Austrian Airlines in February of this year, eleven states of the European Civil Aviation Conference (ECAC), all of which are Member States of ICAO, officially requested the convening of an Extraordinary Session of the ICAO Assembly, the Organization's supreme deliberative

73

organ, to take up the question of international air safety. One of the items on the agenda of the Seventeenth (Extraordinary) Assembly which met in Montreal June 16-30, was:

"consideration of arrangements under which those responsible for criminal actions endangering civil air transport can be brought to justice".

The United Kingdom Delegation to the Assembly presented a Working Paper under this item, entitled "Proposal for an International Convention on Violence Against Aircraft". This question was studied in the Assembly's Committee B (legal matters) and eventually Resolution A17-20, "Proposed Convention on Acts of Unlawful Interference Against International Civil Aviation", was unanimously passed. This Resolution considered that it was necessary to adopt provisions additional to those of international agreements in force and directed the Council to convene the ICAO Legal Committee not later than November 1970 —

"in order to prepare, as the matter of first priority on its Work Programme, a draft convention on acts of unlawful interference against international civil aviation (other than those covered by the draft Convention on Unlawful Seizure of Aircraft) with a view to adoption of the convention at a diplomatic conference as soon as practicable and, if possible, not later than the summer of 1971".

The Legal Committee met in London from September 29th to October 22, 1970, and completed an initial Draft Convention on acts of unlawful interference against international civil aviation. This Draft Convention proceeds to define the offence: provides for the establishment of jurisdiction; and repeats the Articles of the Draft Convention on Unlawful Seizure relating to prosecution; punishment and extradition. The Committee also adopted a Resolution stating that it was of the view that the Draft instrument was ready for a Diplomatic Conference and recommending that the Council take the appropriate steps to convene it. The Council is expected to consider this question shortly, and it appears likely that the Diplomatic Conference will take place in conjunction with the Eighteenth ICAO Assembly scheduled for Vienna in June 1971.

74

Absence of Enforcement Provisions

The Tokyo Convention (to which Canada and 29 other States were parties, up to the end of October, 1970) does not contain any provision relating to the enforcement of the obligations set out in the instrument itself. Article 24(1) does declare that:

"Any dispute between two or more Contracting States concerning the interpretation or application of this Convention which cannot be settled through negotiation, shall, at the request of one of them, be submitted to arbitration. If within six months from the date of the request for arbitration the Parties are unable to agree on the organization of the arbitration, any one of those Parties may refer the dispute to the International Court of Justice by request in conformity with the Statute of the Court."

However, it is evident that the decision of the International Court of Justice with respect to a dispute so referred to it is not binding. Furthermore, Article 24(2) expressly stipulates:

"Each State may at the time of signature or ratification of this Convention or accession thereto, declare that it does not consider itself bound by the preceding paragraph. The other Contracting States shall not be bound by the preceding paragraph with respect to any Contracting State having made such a reservation."

Neither the Draft Convention on Unlawful Seizure nor the Draft Convention on Unlawful Interference yet contain final clauses—these having been left by the ICAO Legal Committee to the respective Diplomatic Conferences. Nevertheless, it appears most unlikely that the final texts of the two treaties will go beyond the settlement of disputes provision in the Tokyo Convention. In this connection, it is worth noting that there is in effect within ICAO a virtual "gentlemen's agreement" that subsequent international instruments relating to offences against civil aviation should, when dealing with matters specifically covered by the Tokyo Convention, repeat precisely the relevant Articles of that instrument. It is for this reason that, for example, Article 6(1) and (3) which are common to both the Unlawful Interference and Unlawful Seizure Draft Conventions are identical to Article 13(2) and (3) of the Tokyo Convention.

75

Thus, while failure or refusal by Contracting States to implement their obligations under any of the three treaties would, of course, involve them in a breach of international legal obligations, at the present time no penalty would be attached to such breach.

Seventeenth (Extraordinary) Assembly — new initiatives

At the opening session of the Assembly on June 16, 1970, the Canadian Delegation presented for circulation a document entitled Canadian Discussion Paper on Linking Bilateral Air Agreements to ICAO International Conventions Relating to Unlawful Interference with Civil Aviation. The paper stated at the outset:

". . .the growing concern with this matter on the part of the international community is encouraging a general climate of opinion conducive towards the consideration of new steps designed to prevent and deter acts of unlawful interference with international civil aviation. Nevertheless, it is recognized that, in the final analysis, only active international cooperation and a willingness on the part of all States involved in international civil aviation to accept and implement international legal obligations can lead to a resolution of the grave problems which are today threatening air transport throughout the world."

The paper then went on to note the lack of enforcement provisions in the Tokyo Convention and the Draft Convention on Unlawful Seizure. Having thus set out the problem, the document proposed a solution: taking into account the fact that scheduled international air transport is generally based on a framework of bilateral air agreements, the document suggested that directly linking these agreements to ICAO conventions relating to unlawful interference —

"could provide a system of effective sanctions for failure to implement international legal obligations under the conventions. It would also be an effective means of securing the widest possible application of the provisions of these conventions, even with respect to states which, for special or particular reasons, do not wish to become parties to them."

A distinction between existing and future bilateral air agreements is drawn in the Discussion Paper since it is clear that

76

amending the former presents complex and difficult problems. The proposal called for ICAO (in the context of the Working Paper this obviously meant the Assembly) to take a decision requesting Member States to amend all existing bilateral agreements by annexing to them a Special Clause. This Clause, it was suggested, should set out the specific provisions of the Tokyo Convention, and any other relevant ICAO convention in force at the time in question, which imposed obligations relating to unlawful interference. Future agreements were to specifically incorporate the Clause in the body of the instruments themselves. In both instances, the Special Clause would permit either party to suspend operation of the agreement one month after communication of notice to the other party if that other party failed to implement its international legal obligations under the Clause. This right to suspend would over-ride any other provision concerning termination or suspension in existing and future bilateral air agreements.

Bilateral agreements, annexing or incorporating the Special Clause, between two States parties to the Tokyo Convention or to future relevant ICAO conventions, would merely be restating existing international legal obligations while ensuring that a sanction was available for their breach. Where only one or neither State was a party to certain or to none of the ICAO conventions, the Special Clause would be a means of bringing into the general international legal system directed towards preventing and deterring unlawful interference, those States which desired to remain outside the conventional framework. With this point in mind, the Discussion Paper suggested—

"that states may avoid becoming parties to this type of multilateral instrument not because they refuse in principle to accept certain obligations contained therein but because they do not want to undertake such obligations with respect to particular Contracting States. In this case, it would appear that incorporation of the pertinent multilateral provisions in bilateral air agreements with third states may well be acceptable."

The proposal makes clear that implementation of the Special Clause approach would allow any State which had a bilateral air agreement with an "offending State"—a State which was in breach of its international legal obligations as set out in the

Clause — legally to suspend operation of the agreement. The sanction would therefore be available not only to the State directly affected by the action of the offending State but to all States having air agreements with the State in default. Thus, even if implementation of the proposed system was limited to the major providers of international air transport, this would create a certain pressure to ensure an important degree of compliance with conventional obligations. The period of time between communication of notice to suspend and the coming into effect of the suspension would, of course, permit the offending State to rectify the situation. Should it proceed to take the steps necessary to comply with its obligations under the Special Clause, the notice could be withdrawn and there would be no interruption of international air services. However, the original decision whether to take action, that is, whether to formally communicate an intention to suspend, would have to be left up to individual States. Since ICAO has no mandatory powers with respect to enforcement of its resolutions, there could be no element of automaticity in the recommended approach.

The Discussion Paper circulated at the Assembly concluded with the statement:

"An eventual decision by ICAO to accept and endorse the proposal outlined above could constitute an important step towards further developing an effective international legal framework to deter and prevent acts of unlawful interference with international civil aviation and contribute significantly towards the maintenance of international air safety."

The Canadian proposal was referred to Committee B for consideration and was eventually taken up in the context of legal measures to deal with actions endangering civil air transport. In the course of informal discussions and private meetings before the item was reached on Committee B's agenda, it became evident that there was substantial opposition to the Special Clause approach. This opposition can be categorized under three headings: (1) objections against the principle that ICAO be concerned with the question of sanctions for breach of legal obligations; (2) objections against the requirement to amend all existing bilateral air agreements, which in the case of some States involved a substantial number; and (3) objections against the development of a system which could result in the disruption of scheduled international air services and cause significant commercial and economic difficulties. It is noteworthy that both large States possessing major international airlines and small States whose airlines service extended routes over-flying and transiting vast areas of the world had serious reservations about the Canadian proposal. In addition, the Representatives of IATA expressed the view that alteration of the existing international air transport system by super-imposing machinery permitting unilateral suspension of air services could result in serious abuses with adverse commercial effects for many airlines. Strong support for Canada's proposal came only from IFALPA and a small number of Delegations which emphasized that all new and dynamic suggestions designed to meet the increasing threats to air safety should receive careful attention.

Concluding that, despite the Austrian Airlines and Swissair disasters, the time might not yet be ripe to press for an ICAO decision, the Canadian Delegation then proposed a lower-key Draft Resolution which, in effect, would defer consideration of the question. The text of the Draft was as follows:

"THE ASSEMBLY:
RECOGNIZING that scheduled international air transport is generally regulated by bilateral air agreements between States;
CONSCIOUS of the great contribution that the Tokyo Convention on Offences and Certain Other Acts Committed on Board Aircraft and future International Civil Aviation Organization conventions relating to unlawful interference with international civil aviation can make towards preventing and deterring such acts;
NOTES the "Canadian Discussion Paper on Linking Bilateral Air Agreements to ICAO International Conventions Relating to Unlawful Interference With Civil Aviation" contained in A17-WP/49;
REQUESTS the Secretariat to circulate it to Member States for study; and
REQUESTS the Council to refer it to the appropriate body for thorough consideration of the subject matter, in connection with the development of international law to deal with acts of unlawful interference with international civil aviation."

In support of the Resolution, it was argued that the main objective of the original Discussion Paper and of the proposed Resolution was to encourage the examination, by the appropriate body, of a possible new approach towards securing the enforcement of international legal obligations under ICAO conventions relating to unlawful interference. Since scheduled international air transport was generally based on bilateral air agreements, directly linking such agreements to appropriate conventions might be an effective method of providing for a system of penalties which could be invoked against States failing to implement certain obligations; this notwithstanding the fact that amending, even by an annex which would not open to alteration, addition or any other change, the existing provisions of bilateral air agreements, might present difficulties for some States.

In opposing the Canadian proposal, the U.S. delegation noted that, while it shared concern about agreeing on a means to provide effective measures to combat unlawful interference with international civil aviation, several important additional elements were involved. First, for any measure to be effective, concerted action by substantially all States to suspend all air services to an offending State would be required. Second, the best means to achieve this end would be through a multilateral convention which would be binding on all States. Finally, in the view of the American delegation, a bilateral approach would entail serious administrative burders and in the end could be relatively ineffective. The American delegation expressed the hope that if the Assembly decided that a study should be made, these considerations would be taken into account.

The Danish delegation, in sharing the misgivings of the U.S. delegation, professed doubt that ICAO would be able to contribute effectively in this field in which commercial interests were so paramount. ICAO had never interfered in the field of bilateral air agreements and it should not do so in the future.

In the event the Resolution — as proposed by Canada — was passed without opposition by Committee B (although several Delegations declined to participate in the vote or abstained) and was unanimously adopted by the Assembly.

Consideration of the Assembly Resolution by the ICAO Council

During the course of its review of all the Resolutions adopted by the Seventeenth (Extraordinary) Assembly, the Council took up the Resolution on Linking Bilateral Air Agreements to ICAO Conventions at its meeting on July 2. It decided that, in accordance with the first operative paragraph of the Resolution, the Secretariat should circulate the Canadian Discussion Paper to Member States for study. The reactions from States would then assist the Secretariat in documenting the subject and, at a later date, the Council would decide on the question as to what was "the appropriate body" which should thoroughly consider the proposal. The Canadian Paper was eventually distributed to all Member States of ICAO under cover of a State Letter, No. LE 3/21, date August 31.

Special ICAO Council Meetings of September 18, 29 and October 1

In the wake of the hijackings of BOAC, Swissair and TWA airliners to the Jordanian Desert; the hijacking to, and immediate destruction of, a Pan American jumbo jet at Cairo International Airport; and the unsuccessful attempt to hijack an El Al aircraft leaving Amsterdam for New York —all in early September of 1970—the United States requested an immediate special meeting of ICAO's permanent body.

The President of the ICAO Council then convened a special meeting, on September 18, 1970. The Canadian governments attitude to the special meeting was indicated in a special statement on September 17, 1970:

"Following up the Canadian initiative on Linking Bilateral Air Agreements to International Conventions on Unlawful Interference with Civil Aviation at the Extraordinary Assembly of ICAO held in Montreal in June, the Canadian Representatives will be putting forward specific proposals for action by the Council regarding sanctions against countries which do not act effectively against hijackers. In particular, the Council will be asked to take up the question of all Member States of the 119 Member Organization incorporating a new provision in all their bilateral air agreements, which provide the framework for virtually all scheduled international air transport around the world.

This provision would stipulate that the State in which a hijacked aircraft lands must immediately release all crew, passengers and baggage on board and immediately return the plane and cargo to the airline. It would also require that the hijacker be taken into custody and either extradited — generally to the state of registration of the aircraft — or prosecuted for crimes connected with the hijacking. If the landing State refused to comply with these obligations, all other States with air services to or from that State would have the legal right to cut off these services on short notice and in effect quickly institute an aerial blockade against the offending State. Under current international air law, such action would be illegal since bilateral air agreements do not normally permit cutting off air services except after twelve months notification. This special provision would apply to other types of unlawful interference with civil aviation as well as hijacking."

Immediately after the official opening of the meeting, the United States Secretary of Transportation, John Volpe, presented for consideration a Draft Resolution relating to the joint suspension of international civil air transport services to and from any State detaining passengers, crew or aircraft for "international blackmail purposes" or failing "to extradite or prosecute persons committing acts of unlawful seizure for international blackmail purposes".

The Canadian delegation then presented for consideration its own Draft Resolution, in the following terms:

"THE COUNCIL

RECALLING Assembly Resolution A16-37 on the subject of unlawful seizure of aircraft;

NOTING that the Tokyo Convention on Offences and Certain Other Acts Committed on Board Aircraft came into force on 4 December 1969;

NOTING that a Diplomatic Conference has been convened in The Hague, 1-16 December 1970 to consider the adoption of a Convention on Unlawful Seizure of Aircraft;

CONSCIOUS of the fact that the framework of scheduled international civil air transport is based on bilateral air agreements between States;

CALLS on all States:

(1) With respect to all future bilateral air agreements, to incorporate a Special Clause which:

(a) explicitly sets out the provisions relating to unlawful interference with civil aviation contained in the Tokyo Convention on Offences and Certain Other Acts Committed on Board Aircraft and any other ICAO

82

Convention or Protocol in force at the time of conclusion of such bilateral air agreements;

(b) notwithstanding any other provision concerning termination, shall permit either party to suspend operation of the bilateral air agreement one month after communication of notice, if the other party fails to implement the obligations set out in the Special Clause;

(2) With respect to existing bilateral air agreements, to amend them, at the earliest possible time, by means of a Special Clause which:

(a) explicitly sets out the provisions relating to unlawful interference with civil aviation contained in the Tokyo Convention on Offences and Certain Other Acts Committed on Board Aircraft and any other ICAO Convention or Protocol in force at the relevant time;

(b) notwithstanding any other provision concerning termination, shall permit either party to suspend operation of the bilateral air agreement one month after communication of notice, if the other party fails to implement the obligations set out in the Special Clause."

When the ICAO Council resumed its special meeting on September 29, 1970, it was officially advised by the United States and Canadian representatives of various changes in their respective Draft Resolutions. The revised Canadian Draft Resolution incorporated two Preambular paragraphs in addition to those in the original:

"FURTHER RECALLING Assembly Resolution A17-23 concerning the Discussion Paper on Linking Bilateral Air Agreements to Certain ICAO International Conventions;" and

"FURTHER NOTING that the 18th Session of the Legal Committee has been directed to draft a convention on acts of unlawful interference against international civil aviation (other than those covered by the draft Convention on Unlawful Seizure of Aircraft);"

The operative section was completely altered to read:

"DIRECTS the Legal Committee, at its 18th Session:

(1) to elaborate a Special Clause providing for the enforcement of international legal obligations relating to unlawful interference with international civil aviation which could be:

(a) specifically incorporated in future bilateral air agreements between Member States; and

(b) inserted in existing bilateral air agreements at an appropriate time; and

(2) to transmit the text of the Special Clause, together with its Report on the relevant discussions, to the ICAO Council at the earliest possible date, so that the Council may consider what recommendations to make to Member States with regard to the Clause."

Detailed debate on the proposals then took place in the Council with the Representatives of Tunisia and Lebanon, in particular, taking a strong line in opposition to ICAO's competence with respect to sanctions. In the event both Draft Resolutions were again slightly amended, before their adoption by the Council, the following amendment to the Canadian text having been proposed by the Representative of the Federal Republic of Germany and accepted by Canada:

"DIRECTS the Legal Committee, at its 18th Session:
(1) to consider whether a Special Clause could be elaborated . . . and
(2) to transmit the text of any Special Clause that may be elaborated . . ."

The final votes on the two Resolutions were: the USA proposal — 14 in favour (including Canada), 3 against (Lebanon, Tunisia and the UAR) and 10 abstentions; on the Canadian proposal — 18 in favour, 0 against and 6 abstentions, with 3 Representatives (Lebanon, Tunisia and the UAR) not participating.

After nearly three days of thorough discussion and occasionally heated debate, the Council had thus decided to refer the question of sanctions — in the context of the American and Canadian initiatives — to the ICAO Legal Committee which was authorized, if necessary, to extend its Eighteenth Session which had been convened for London, beginning on September 24, 1970, (on the Unlawful Interference with Aircraft Draft Convention).

ICAO Legal Committee Consideration of the Second Council Resolution of October 1

Before the item concerning the two Council Resolutions had yet been reached on the Legal Committee's agenda, the Canadian Delegation circulated a "Canadian Working Paper on Securing Enforcement of International Legal Obligations Relating to Unlawful Interference with International Civil Aviation by Means of Incorporating a Special Clause in Bilateral Air Agreements". This document briefly outlined the history of the Special Clause approach and then stated:

84

"The Canadian Delegation is of the view that the special clause should set out basic obligations relating to:

(a) Immediate release of all members of the crew, all passengers and all baggage on board an aircraft which has been the subject of unlawful seizure or other interference, and to immediately return to persons lawfully entitled to possession aircraft, cargo and mail (based on Article 11 of the Tokyo Convention and Article 9 of the draft convention on unlawful seizure);

(b) taking into immediate custody persons alleged to be responsible for the act of unlawful seizure or interference for sufficient time as is reasonably necessary to enable extradition or criminal proceedings to be instituted (based on Article 6 of the draft convention on unlawful seizure); and

(c) either: (i) extradition of persons alleged to be responsible for the act of unlawful seizure or interference to the State of Registration of the aircraft or to such other State as has, and wished to exercise, jurisdiction or,
(ii) initiation of criminal proceedings against persons alleged responsible for the act of unlawful seizure or interference.

The clause would thus stipulate that, notwithstanding any other termination or suspension provision in the bilateral air agreement, in the event one party failed to implement the obligations set out in the Clause, the other party would be permitted to suspend the operation of the agreement (or alternatively, to suspend international air transport services governed by the agreement) on 15 days notice."

It will be noted that the language used is much stronger than that of the Tokyo Convention and the Draft Convention on Unlawful Seizure relating to release of passengers and return of aircraft, and that the effective date of suspension after notification had been reduced from one month to fifteen days. For purposes of discussion in the Committee and to allow a certain degree of flexibility in the eventual elaboration of a Special Clause, it was apparent that an initially strongly-worded draft had a number of advantages.

The Committee was, however, faced with an immediate problem when it finally turned its attention to the ICAO Council Resolution. With only limited time available, it had to consider two complex and difficult proposals. To assist the Committee to give adequate attention to both matters and to ensure that the various aspects of the Special Clause approach were examined in detail, the Canadian Delegation proposed the establishment of a Working Group. The Canadian Delegation's view was that after a relatively short time, the Working Group should be in a position to report to the Committee Chairman on the progress it had made, the report to be distributed to all Delegations, following which a suitable period of time could be set aside in Plenary (which would have meanwhile taken up the first Council Resolution) for the consideration of its contents.

It soon became evident that the majority of the members of the Legal Committee did not believe that the Legal Committee as a whole could come to any specific conclusions on either of the two proposals referred to it by the Council. Documentation was not complete; there had been almost no time for study and reflection. Most important, representatives did not have detailed instructions from their Governments. The Canadian Delegation then presented a further Working Paper entitled "Suggestions Relating to the Organization of Work Concerning the Second Resolution Adopted by the Council on October 1, 1970". After reviewing the Second Resolution of October 1, the Paper declared:

"The Delegation of Canada firmly believes that the most progress would be achieved with respect to the Committee's work relating to this Resolution, if the subject matter could be referred to a working group of approximately eight members, composed of — perhaps — representatives of three delegations from Asia and Africa, three from North and South America and two from Europe. The Canadian Delegation is of the view that, after appropriate consultations with various delegations, the Chairman would be in a position to appoint the members of the working group.

This body should be given an initial mandate to:
(1) study the legal feasibility of elaborating the kind of Special Clause envisaged in the Council Resolution. This study would take into account the general nature and form of bilateral air agreements, and the usual provisions contained in them relating to their amendment; and the meaning to be attached to, and scope of, the term "unlawful interference".
(2) ascertain the particular problems involved in elaborating such a Special Clause. These would include the manner in which each party to a bilateral air agreement would undertake vis-à-vis the other party specific obligations arising from the consequences of unlawful acts directed against foreign international civil air transport; and the possible effect on the bilateral air agreement of a breach of these obligations, that is whether to provide for suspension of only inter-

national civil air transport services to and from the offending state or the suspension of operation of the entire bilateral agreement;

(3) consider what specific international legal obligations should be included in the Special Clause. In this connection reference would be made to the relevant provisions of the Tokyo Convention on Offences and Certain Other Acts Committed on Board Aircraft, the draft convention on unlawful seizure of aircraft, and the work just accomplished on a draft unlawful interference convention.

The working group should endeavour to provide a report on its discussions to the Committee not later than three days before the conclusion of the current Legal Committee sitting. Plenary would then be in a position to decide as to what further action should be taken to carry out the instructions of the Council."

Eventually, it was unanimously agreed that the Working Group should be established. The Working Group, — composed of Representatives of Canada, Belgium, Brazil, France, Netherlands, the United Kingdom and the U.S.A., with attendance by Observers from New Zealand, Italy, and IFALPA, — held four meetings. As had been decided by the Legal Committee, the terms of reference were based on the second Canadian Working Paper mentioned above.

The Canadian Delegation then presented for distribution a third Working Paper setting out "for the guidance of the Working Group" a Draft text of a Special Clause. As submitted, the Draft Special Clause reads as follows:

"In order to further the objective of promoting the safe and orderly development of international air transport services;

And to deter and prevent acts of violence and other unlawful acts or omissions directed against international civil air transport;

A. Each Contracting Party undertakes to fulfill the following obligations at such time as an aircraft which has been the object of unlawful seizure or other act of unlawful interference, or passengers or crew on board such aircraft, are present in its territory as a result of unlawful seizure or other act of unlawful interference:

(1) to permit the passengers and crew of the aircraft, to continue their journey without delay;

(2) to return the aircraft, cargo and mail to the persons lawfully entitled to possession;

(3) to take into immediate custody, in accordance with national law, the person or persons alleged to be responsible for the act of unlawful seizure or other act of unlawful interference for such period of time as is reasonably necessary to enable extradition or criminal proceedings to be instituted against such person or persons; and

(4) either

(a) to extradite such person or persons to the state of registration of the aircraft which has been the object of unlawful seizure or other act of unlawful interference, or to some other state which has, and wishes to exercise, jurisdiction over such person or persons or

(b) to initiate criminal proceedings against such person or persons in respect of the unlawful seizure or other act of unlawful interference.

B. Notwithstanding any other provision relating to the settlement of disputes, suspension of operation or termination of the present agreement, in the event either Contracting Party fails to fulfill any of the obligations set out in Part A of this clause, the other Contracting Party may, at any time prior to the fulfillment of such obligation, give notice that it desires to suspend the operation of the present agreement. Such notice shall be simultaneously communicated to the first Contracting Party and to the Secretary General of ICAO. Suspension of operation of all provisions of the present agreement, other than the provision relating to the settlement of disputes, shall be effective (15) days after the date of receipt of the notice, unless the notice to suspend is withdrawn before the expiry of this period. In the absence of acknowledgement of receipt by the Contracting Party to which notice has been given, notice shall be deemed to have been received 7 days after its receipt by the Secretary General of ICAO."

On October 21, 1970, the Working Group submitted its Report to the parent Committee. On the subject of "Legal Feasibility of a Special Clause", the Report stated:

"The Working Group agreed that it was legally feasible for States to include, by mutual agreement, into their bilateral agreements on air services a Special Clause contemplated in the second resolution adopted by the ICAO Council on 1 October 1970. The purpose of such clause would be to give a party the right to suspend the operation of certain provisions of a bilateral air agreement between the two Contracting States and would in no way affect the applicability of the provisions of other (multilateral) treaties, such as Article 5 of the Chicago Convention, Air Services Transit Agreement, etc.

It was noted that the framework of bilateral air agreements is essentially commercial and that it is unusual in the present practice to introduce such special clauses relating to enforcement of certain international legal obligations not covered by the subject matter of the agreement. However, the Clause as contemplated would be a mutual obligation freely entered into and in the view of some members it would not thus be a "penal" provision or a "sanction". The Clause would only provide, on bilateral basis, mechanism for enforcement of provisions contained in the Clause itself."

Under the heading "Particular Problems Involved in Elaborating the Special Clause", the Report went on:

"Among the particular problems involved in elaborating a Special Clause the following were considered by the Working Group:

(a) Would the Clause be applicable even if the parties to the bilateral agreement or one of them were not parties to the Tokyo Convention, Convention on Unlawful Seizure and Convention on Unlawful Interference? The Working Group agreed that States are free, on a bilateral basis, to accept as between themselves the principles of multilateral conventions to which they are not parties. The Working Group considered the related question as to whether, and how, the Clause would be applicable to a case involving a third State. The following example was considered: States A and B would insert into their bilateral air agreement the Special Clause; State B would detain aircraft of State C after an unlawful seizure; State B has no legal obligation to State C because neither State B nor C are parties to Tokyo Convention or Convention on Unlawful Seizure; could the State A suspend the operation of the bilateral agreement with State B in such a situation? The Working Group recognized that problems such as the absence of any extradition arrangements between States B and C, and the lack of jurisdiction over the offence on the part of State B, might exist, however, it reached no conclusion on this issue.

(b) While the Working Group noted that some States not parties to a multilateral Convention might possibly accept some of the multilateral obligations in a bilateral air agreement, doubt was expressed as to whether the bilateral air agreement approach would contribute substantially to widespread acceptance of these obligations.

(c) A question was raised whether one State may unilaterally, within the framework of a bilateral agreement, judge the behaviour of the other State with respect to the application of its national law. It was pointed out, however, that the settlement of disputes procedure in the agreement would remain in force and thus the State allegedly in default would have a remedy in respect of any abuse of the Special Clause by the State invoking it. However, the Working Group recognized that the settlement of disputes procedure would normally take some time and may not thus provide an effective remedy for the State alleged to be in default.

(d) The efficacy of the Special Clause would depend, to a large degree, on concerted international co-operation; collective action by a number of States might well be essential. The Working Group considered it worth exploring the possibility of including the Canadian proposal into some multilateral scheme (e.g. by a multilateral agreement so that the Special Clause would be automatically applicable between any two States parties to that multilateral agreement, whether or not the international air services between those two

States were dependent upon a bilateral air agreement. Parties to this agreement should also be obliged to use their best endeavours to include the Special Clause into their bilateral agreements with States not parties to the multilateral agreement). It was felt that such a scheme could also provide for a machinery for joint determination whether there was a default (see (c) above), joint action and common machinery for the settlement of differences. (It was pointed out that in the absence of a common machinery for arbitration different arbitral tribunals may render divergent arbitral awards on the same incident).

(e) The question was raised how long should the suspension of air services last and when and following what procedure would the services be resumed. Two possibilities were mentioned:

(i) the services should be suspended only for the period while the default (e.g. detention of aircraft) lasts,

(ii) the services should remain suspended until the issue is finally settled by arbitration. On this issue an opinion was expressed that this alternative would, in fact, be a sanction not justified by concern for safety.

The Working Group has not reached any conclusion on this issue.

(f) The Working Group agreed that if the Canadian approach were adopted, it would be desirable to have a uniform *standard* Special Clause which would be incorporated in all bilateral agreements. The Working Group noted, however, that ICAO sponsorship of the Special Clause would be recommendatory only and hence, States would, in principle, be free to vary the language of the Special Clause from one bilateral to another."

Turning to "Specific Legal Obligations to be Included in the Special Clause", the document had this to say:

"The Working Group believed that the enumeration of the specific legal obligations in the Special Clause should follow the language of the three Convention (Tokyo, Unlawful Seizure and Unlawful Interference). The Clause should be *standard* (see paragraph 5(f) above); the majority of the Working Group were of the view that any endeavours to make the obligations under the Clause stricter than the obligations under the three Conventions might not be successful. Doubts were expressed whether all acts enumerated in Article 1 of the Draft Convention on Unlawful Interference should be covered by the Special Clause; some of these acts could be of pure national nature and may possibly not justify the suspension of the air services. The view was expressed that only the major offences should be mentioned in the Special Clause.

The Working Group noted that there could be a different approach and a different procedure for suspension of services in case of

(a) detention of aircraft, passengers and crew (here the aspects of threat to safety are more prominent) and

90

(b) failure by a State to extradite or punish the perpetrator of the offence in accordance with its national law or international obligations (here the urgency and the concern of the international community may be lesser and arbitration may precede the suspension of services).

A question was raised whether the Special Clause should also mention return of *mail* (separately from cargo). Although bilateral air agreements generally mention passengers, cargo and mail, it was pointed out that the Tokyo Convention only mentions cargo as the restitution of mail is already covered by Convention of the UPU. However, it was agreed that it might be useful to specifically include reference to mail into the Special Clause.

There was a consensus in the Working Group that the Special Clause should provide only for suspension of air transport services and not for suspension of other provisions of the bilateral agreement."

And, on "Efficacy of the Special Clause", the Report observed that:

"The Special Clause would not cover the operations under Article 5 of the Chicago Convention and under the International Air Services Transit Agreement.

It may be difficult to obtain a general agreement of States to insert the Special Clause into their bilateral agreements.

The process of amending bilateral agreements may be extremely time-consuming. In some countries the modifications will have to be ratified through parliamentary procedure.

Also, in some cases this amending process may lead to renegotiation on other aspects of the bilateral agreement."

Added on to this was the tentative conclusion that:

"A multilateral approach to the Special Clause to be included into bilateral air agreements may be a solution to the practical problems set out above."

Finally, the Report recommended that:

"The Canadian proposal (bilateral approach) and U.S. proposal (multilateral approach) should be further studied by a Subcommittee of the Legal Committee at an early date; this Subcommittee should have the benefit of this Report, comments of States on the documentation relating to, and discussion which took place at, the 18th Session of the Legal Committee."

During the course of its preliminary consideration of the first Council Resolution, the Legal Committee had concluded that it would have to refer the general question of a new Draft

"Convention Regarding the Safety and Security of International Civil Air Transport Services" (the text of which was formally proposed by the U.S.A. Representative on October 15, 1970) to a Special Subcommittee for careful study. Eventually, the Committee decided by a vote of 22 to 0, with 2 abstentions, to establish such a body to undertake a detailed examination of both the American and Canadian proposals "in the light of opinions expressed in the Committee at this session, and to make recommendations with respect to these proposals."

Before concluding the Eighteenth Session on October 22, the Committee adopted a Resolution noting the Report of the Working Group on the Special Clause approach and a Report (prepared by an informal Drafting Group composed of Representatives of a number of Delegations) on the new U.S.A. Draft Convention. These documents, the minutes of the Session and the relevant Working Papers will provide the basis for the Special Sub-Committee's deliberations at such time as it will be constituted. The chairman of the Legal Committee is at present engaging in consultations with Representatives from various Member States with a view to agreeing on its composition. While the Committee made no decision as to when the Sub-Committee should meet, it did adopt by a narrow one vote majority, 7 (including Canada) to 6 with 10 abstentions, a Netherlands proposal, offering facilities at The Hague before or after the Unlawful Seizure Conference in December, 1970.

Conclusion

It now remains for the Special Sub-Committee to be established and to begin a comprehensive study of both the U.S.A. and Canadian initiatives, and especially the issue of the incorporation of the Special Clause approach in a multilateral framework. The arguments in favour of adopting the Special Clause approach can be summarised as follows. It could be proceeded with entirely separate from, and even complementary to, a multilateral approach (once the Clause was elaborated and approved, there would be no financial or adminis-

92

trative implications as far as ICAO was concerned, no need for a Diplomatic Conference). Again, it would provide a "legal mechanism" for dealing with the situation preceding and pending the coming into force of any relevant multilateral convention or protocol; for bringing into any general multilateral system, which may be devised, those States which, for various reasons, are not likely to become parties to the specific multilateral instrument, and providing them with a legal means for overriding provisions of bilateral air agreements which could not otherwise be suspended or terminated; and, finally, for laying the groundwork for dealing effectively with hijackings and other acts of unlawful interference with international civil aviation which do not involve international blackmail or other activities which may be provided for in a multilateral instrument.

The goal is evident and obvious — prevention and deterrence of unlawful interference with international civil aviation by the development of an effective international legal system. The means remain undecided, whether a multilateral convention providing for mandatory sanctions against States in default; or widespread adoption of a Special Clause amending bilateral air agreements to permit suspension of services to and from offending States; or a combination of both? ICAO must now proceed to answer this question — as a matter of urgency. The world aviation organization must accept the challenge and the responsibility thus thrust upon it by international public opinion, by governments which look to it for direction and guidance in air transportation matters and, above all, by the international aviation community which provides and supports international air services.

ADDENDUM

Implementation of an International Enforcement System

by L.S. Clark

Major steps along the road to developing an effective legal framework to prevent and deter acts of unlawful interference against international civil air transport are now being accomplished. As a result of two ICAO Council Resolutions adopted on October 1, 1970, the Organization's Legal Committee extended its 18th Session in London in October, 1970, by some ten days to take up the question of sanctions and enforcement of international legal obligations relating to unlawful interference. Two proposals were under study: a United States initiative on an international Convention Regarding the Safety and Security of International Civil Air Transport Services; and a Canadian initiative on linking bilateral air agreements to certain ICAO conventions by means of annexing a special clause.

In the event that some generally acceptable and widely applied international enforcement system be developed, many serious problems remain nevertheless with respect to its implementation. This will be the case whether the eventual system itself be based upon a multilateral convention; upon the amending of bilateral air agreements; or upon a combination of both. In the main, there would appear to be three key issues involved.

The first issue is as to the method for organizing and establishing the kind of particular international co-operation required to secure agreement to effect sanctions against an offending State. The offending State, here, is a State in default of particular international legal obligations. It will be evident that when some incident such as a hijacking and the subsequent detention of passengers, crew, or the aircraft itself takes place, there will be a number of States with a special interest in the case. These will include, but are not necessarily limited to, the State of registration or operation of the aircraft; the State from which the aircraft took off before it was hijacked (and perhaps the State to which it was headed); and the States of nationality of the passengers on board. There must be some general framework within which these States can operate to consider the incident and, if it be so decided, to regulate the imposition of sanctions. (These "sanctions" will usually involve the suspension of international air services to and from the offending State.) An international convention can, of course, provide for consultation machinery and even set out a process for decision-making with respect to the suspension of international air services. Nevertheless, the drawbacks of any multilateral system would still apply. These include the unlikelihood that certain States will become a party to the treaty and, accordingly, refuse to take part in the consultations and the difficulty in ascertaining all the "interested" States. (How does one rapidly verify the fact that a national of a particular State indeed was or was not on board, and what of persons of dual nationality?) A bilateral air agreement system is perhaps easier, since all States which are parties to such agreements with the offending State would automatically be brought into the consultations. There remains, however, the problem as to how a decision to suspend services is to be made. Would it be by majority vote, based on weighted voting, or must it be unanimous?

The second issue relates to *communication and co-ordination between the responsible national authorities and their international airlines and other air transport facilities* which will be affected by the suspension of services. This, of course, will be a matter of individual domestic law and regulation and may require amendments to such laws and regulations so that a given State may be in a position to give effect to any relevant international decisions. One can imagine several complicating factors. The airline which normally flies to the so-called "offending" State may have already sold large numbers of air tickets to prospective travellers to that destination; scheduled

95

flights to other areas of the world may involve stop-overs in that State flights to which are now to be suspended; suspension of services may not affect rights under article 5 of the Chicago Convention or the Air Services Transit Agreement. Thus, the air carrier and the respective Ministries of Civil Aviation or Transport, etc. would have to have co-ordination machinery so that the international obligation to impose sanctions undertaken by the Government can be implemented through the airline and other appropriate civil air transport facilities.

The third major issue involves the *resumption of air services to and from the State which has rectified its erstwhile status of having been in default of its international legal obligations.* Who is to judge when a State is no longer in default, and when will services be resumed? A multilateral treaty could, of course, specifically include provisions relating to this, and so could a bilateral air agreement system. However, these may not be definitive in nature and there could easily be disagreement among the "interested" States as to whether or not the offending State is still in default. Also, and this is an extremely important consideration, commercial and economic interests may become more and more significant as the length of time during which services are suspended grows longer. If any one State amongst the group engaging in concerted action should opt, of its own initiative, to resume services, the solid front on which any sanctions systems depends will have been broken. How can this be prevented? The foregoing discussion raises some of the serious issues concerning effective implementation of any enforcement system. It is clear that while it may be easy to point out the problems, the solutions are far more difficult to attain.

Chapter 6

PUNITION INTERNATIONALE DE L'ACTUELLE PIRATERIE AÉRIENNE

par Haroldo Valladao

Le monde est hanté actuellement par le *nouvel essor* d'un crime néfaste: la piraterie, soit en mer, p. ex. le cas célèbre du navire portugais *Santa Maria*, dans la mer des Caraibes et de l'Atlantique sud, de Caracas à Recife, en 1961, et récemment du bateau de plaisance américain, *Jack Rogers*, de Miami à Cuba, en février 1970, et du transport de munitions de la flotte des Etats Unis, *Columbia Eagle*, naviguant vers la Thailande, détourné au Cambodge en mars 1970; *soit dans l'espace* avec de fréquents assauts perpetrés contre des avions, commencés en 1961, sur un vol Mexicain pour Cuba, et jusqu'au transport par chemin de fer, avec un train détourné aux Etats Unis en décembre 1970.

C'est un délit qui exige une punition exemplaire et des poursuites internationales, comme cela a toujours été depuis le Droit Romain et particulièrement lorsque le crime se répand, comme on l'observe maintenant, de même qu'aux XVe et XVIIe Siècles. Dans ce sens, *Ortolan* a écrit en 1853: "Dans tous les temps et toutes les nations, la justice humaine s'est armée d'une grande sévérité contre le crime de piraterie" (*Règles Internationales et Diplomatie de la Mer*, 1, p. 235).

La piraterie est essentiellement, assaut, attentat, déprédation, violence, banditisme, violation de la vie, de l'intégrité, de la liberté et de la sécurité des hommes et des communications, soit sur terre, l'ancien pillage des grandes routes non surveillées, soit sur mer et, particulièrement en haute mer, où en l'absence d'un pouvoir juridictionnel, il existe un champ encore plus propice aux criminels.

Le droit international a donc été obligé de reconnaître aux Etats le droit de police et juridiction sur la piraterie en haute mer (1) et les Etats mêmes ont été obligés de la punir par leurs lois internes dénombrant les formes différentes qu'elle présente, et allant jusqu'à la peine de mort, appliquée même en flagrant délit.

C'est un crime contre l'humanité et pour cela, les pirates ont été appelés ennemis du genre humain, "hosti humani generis": (en 1935 encore, ils étaient ainsi qualifiés par le Judicial Committee of the Privy Council).

Or, aujourd'hui, la piraterie, non seulement sévit en mer dans les cas cités ci-dessus, n. 1 et plusieurs autres en Extrême-Orient, mais obéissant à sa tendance *traditionnelle de rechercher les endroits isolés*, dépourvus de police, s'est attaquée à la *navigation aérienne*, de "sive mari sive terra" (Bynkershoeck) aussi à "sive aere" ou "coele", dans la forme actuelle de capture d'un aéronef privé en vol par une personne à bord qui empêche son exploitation, qui s'empare de cet aéronef ou exerce son contrôle, ou est prête à exécuter ces actions.

La punition de ce crime, *d'intérêt universel*, surpasse une seule branche du droit: elle n'appartient pas seulement au droit pénal, ni d'une manière restreinte au droit maritime ou au droit aérien. Elle appartient en plein au droit international.

Ce crime a des horizons propres et amples. C'est un problème autonome où des *normes internationales et pénales doivent être intégrées*, en considérant les données fournies par le droit maritime et le droit aérien. Le juriste qui l'étudie ne peut pas être limité ou encadré par l'un ou l'autre de ses contours.

Le droit international sur la piraterie est dépassé, exigeant de grandes reformes (V. le travail du Prof. *D.N.H. Johnson*, présenté à la 8ème Session de la International Law Comm., du 23 avril au 4 juin 1956, et celui de *H. Valladao* in "The Freedom of the Air", Edward McWhinney and M.A. Bradley, editors (1968) pages 223-234).

Le droit international ne punit pas la piraterie et *n'oblige pas les Etats* à la prévoir comme un crime et à établir la punition appropriée. Il ne la prévoit que pour des buts juridictionnels.

Classiquement, selon une règle coutumière de droit international, par exception au principe de la liberté de navigation en haute mer, les Etats avaient *le droit de procéder à la visite des navires soupçonnés de piraterie et à la capture de ceux qui la pratiquaient*, en jugeant les pirates, considérés hors du droit international, *selon les lois sur la piraterie de l'Etat du navire qui les a capturés. C'était une faculté et non une obligation*. Dans ce sens, la décision du Judicial Committee of the Privy Council, de 1935, et le travail de la Harvard Law School (American Journal of International Law, Volume 26, 769/70) et les articles 14 et 19 de la convention de Genève sur la Haute Mer du 25/4/1958 sont définitifs.

Mais si cette convention a marqué un progrès en prévoyant aussi la piraterie aérienne, elle a été très restrictive en donnant la définition de piraterie maritime et aérienne (avec les protestations, par ex. de la délégation de l'URSS), exigeant pour caractériser les actes de piraterie *qu'ils partent d'un navire ou aéronef contre un autre navire ou aéronef* (voyez l'excellent travail du Professeur de la Faculté de Droit de Oviedo, Espagne, Dr. *José Perez Montero* "La Literatura Juridica relativa al caso del Santa Maria", (1963).

La convention écarte donc le cas célèbre du navire *Santa Maria*, capturé en haute mer avec usage de la violence, par le passager Galvao et d'autres individus qui ont changé la route et la destination du navire mais qui n'ont pas pratiqué des actes de pillage *contre d'autres navires; elle écarte, par conséquent, les autres cas identiques et courants de piraterie maritime et aérienne*.

De plus, la Convention de Genève n'exige pas et ne détermine pas que les Etats punissent la *piraterie*, elle n'établit pas qu'ils doivent prévoir et punir le crime de piraterie dans leurs Codes et Lois, comme le font les conventions Internationales sur les délits internationaux, "juris gentium" par ex., les attentats contre des cables sous-marins, le trafic des femmes et enfants, le commerce et les actes visant à faciliter l'usage de stupéfiants, le génocide ... L'article 14 de la Convention se limite à disposer que les Etats doivent coopérer dans toute la mesure du possible pour la répression de la piraterie et *seulement en haute mer ou en quelque autre endroit hors de la juridiction d'un Etat.* Et pour cela, les Etats ne sont pas considérés comme devant la punir spécialement dans leur droit interne.

Moins dépassés, bien qu'antérieurs à cette Convention, sont les traités plurilatéraux. Celui de Droit Pénal International de Montevideo, 1889, art. 13, et 1940, art. 14, et celui de la Havane (Code Bustamante, 1928) art. 308, 1928, ont établi comme principe général que la piraterie et d'autres délits internationaux, quel que soit le lieu où ils sont commis (Montevideo, 1940), en haute mer, dans l'espace libre et dans des territoires non organisés en Etats (Havane), sont punis par l'Etat auteur de la capture, *sous réserve de la sollicitation d'extradition par l'Etat dans lequel le délit a été consommé* (Montevideo, 1940). Ils considèrent, *sagement*, la *piraterie comme un délit international*, bien que sans en avoir donné la définition appropriée.

Encore moins dépassée est l'enseignement de Oppenheim: "If the crew, or passengers, revolt on the open sea and convert the vessel and her goods to their own use, they commit piracy, whether the vessel is private or public. But a simple act of violence on the part of crew or passengers does not constitute in itself the crime of piracy, at least not as far as International Law is concerned. If, for instance, the crew were to murder the master on account of his cruelty and afterwards carried on the voyage, they would be murderers but not pirates. They are pirates only if the revolt is directed, not merely against the master, but also against the vessel for the purpose of converting her and her goods to their own use" (International Law, Vol. I, 8th ed. by Lauterpacht, (1955), § 274, page 614). Voyez aussi Colombos, qui écrit: "Piratical acts may be of different kinds. If the crew and or passengers of a vessel revolt and seek by armed force to convert the ship or cargo to their own use; if a ship stops another and forcibly removes passengers and holds them for ransom, or if persons on board are killed though the vessel is released, it is still piracy. If the master and officers are compelled to steer the vessel by command of the rebels to a place where they can pilfer her, it is also piracy. The 'Hi-jackers' who prey on 'rum-runners' off some coasts of America are pirates" (International Law of the Sea (6th ed., 1967), § 459, page 445). Et aux Etats-Unis dans

100

le même sens *Bishop*: "Moreover, the mariners may commit piracy upon it; if they shall violently dispossess the master and afterwards carry away the ship itself or any of the goods or tackle, apparel or funiture, feloniously." And the passengers doing the same incur the like guilt: (New Criminal Law, (8th ed., 1892), Vol. 3, page 618).

Dans le droit interne, dans les Codes et Lois Pénales des Etats sur la piraterie, la définition du crime est plus ample que celle donnée par le droit international, en premier lieu parce qu'elle prévoit le crime et prescrit la punition appropriée et, en deuxième lieu, parce qu'elle donne une définition plus large du crime cité.

Le droit interne présente, donc, une *caractérisation* plus *étendue du crime*, en considérant la *piraterie*, également comme *l'appropriation par fraude ou violence contre le commandant, d'un navire, soit par un individu appartenant à l'équipage* (Lois Française du 10 avril 1825, *Piraterie*, art. 4ème, n. 1, du Brésil, *Pirateria*, Code Criminel de l'Empire, 1830, art. 82, n. 3, et Pénal de la République, art. 104, § 3ème), *soit par une personne quelconque, incluant les passagers*, Espagne, *Pirateria*, Code Pénal, 1848, art. 250, Italie, Code de Marine Marchande, 1877, *Pirateria*, arts. 327 et 333, Codes Pénales Hispano-Américains, *Pirateria*, Bolivie, 1834, art. 166, 3ème, Honduras, 1906, 137, 3ème, Paraguay, 1910, 144, 3ème, Uruguay, 142, 3ème, Argentine, 1921, 198, 3ème, Perou, 1924, 271, 3ème, Cuba, Code de Défense Sociale, Liberté et Sûreté des Mers, art. 168, O et 196, C (appropriation d'un navire ou *aéronef* cubain). Dans cette législation évidemment sont prévus comme piraterie les cas des navires Santa Maria (passagers), Jack Rogers (assaillant) et Columbia Eagle (matelots) et d'une façon correlative, ceux des avions depuis 1961.

Aussitôt après le premier cas d'avion détourné de sa route, un aéronef de la Panamerican, le 9 aout 1961, en vol du Mexique pour Cuba, les Etats Unis ont approuvé une loi le 5 septembre 1961 prévoyant et punissant le crime sous le titre de "Aircraft Piracy" avec des peines allant de 20 ans de prison jusqu'à la mort. Le Mexique, en demandant l'extradition de l'auteur de ce crime l'a qualifié de *pirateria*, en se fondant sur le Traité de l'Extradition respectif du 25 mai 1925 (art. 2ème) qui l'y autorisait dans les cas de *pirateria,* selon le Droit International.

Le 30 octobre 1961, dans une réunion de la Section brésilienne de l'Association Internationale de Droit Pénal, à Rio de Janeiro, j'ai mis la question de la piraterie aérienne sur le tapis, avec l'appui de l'éminent juriste pénal latino-américain, qu'est le Professeur *Sebastian Soler*, lequel dans la réforme du Code Pénal de l'Argentine, effectuée par la Loi 17.657 (1/4/1968) l'a *prévue comme piraterie* afin que: "El que mediante violencia, intimidacion o engano, usurpar de la autoridad de un buque o aeronave con el fin de apoderarse de el a de las cosas e personas que lleva". Dans un même but le Code du Mexique a été modifié par une loi du 24/12/1968, qui prévoit le délit.

Il faut noter qu'au Portugal, après ce qui arriva au navire Santa Maria, comme la loi portugaise ne prévoyait pas le cas de piraterie par appropriation du bateau, un Décret-loi du 21/2/1962, *a modifié l'article 162 du Code Pénal pour y inclure soit la capture au moyen de fraude ou violence*, d'un navire ou aéronef (§ 1er), soit l'usurpation du commandement, de navires ou d'aéronefs nationaux, ou affrétés par une société nationale . . . (§ 3ème).

Finalement, la Loi Cubaine, n. 1226 du 19 septembre 1969, en règlant le sujet, a élargi le contour de sa législation citée, qui ne punissait que la piraterie contre navires et aéronefs cubains, pour l'étendre à un *navire ou aéronef* quelconque, prévoyant, spécifiquement, dans l'article 1er le crime pour les actes de capturer, soustraire ou s'approprier une *nef aérienne ou maritime par un moyen quelconque* (lettre a) détourner une nef aérienne ou maritime de sa route ou de ses activités normales . . . (lettre b) mettre en péril la sûreté d'une nef aérienne ou maritime . . . (lettre c). Selon certaines informations, Cuba aurait déjà puni de cinq années d'emprisonnement celui qui n'agissait pas pour des raisons politiques.

Il faut observer l'union, dans les Conventions Internationales citées, *Code Bustamante*, art. 308, et de *Genève* arts. 15 et suivants, des deux pirateries, la maritime et l'aérienne.

Et en plus marqué et plus efficaces, plusieurs lois internes citées, surtout celles des dernières années *mettant la forme actuelle de piraterie aérienne dans le même texte que la*

102

piraterie maritime, prévoyent ainsi, la punition des pirates de la mer et de l'air, de ceux qui s'emparent d'un navire ou d'un aéronef, en usurpant le commandement, en le détournant de sa route, etc.

En vérité, on ne peut pas punir seulement la capture illicite d'un aéronef et laisser impunies, comme dans le cas du *Santa Maria ou du Columbia Eagle*, la capture d'un bateau ou, comme dans le cas du bateau *Jack Rogers*, la simple tentative.

La prévision du crime et sa punition doivent être incluses dans le même texte conventionnel ou légal.

Quant à la dénomination de piraterie pour les crimes actuels de capture violente et de détournement de navires et aéronefs, les deux uniques membres du Comité de la International Law Association qui se sont manifestés à ce sujet, *étaient, d'accord pour maintenir le terme piraterie, et ont répudié, formellement, l'expression "hi-jacking"*.

Dans un rapport préliminaire à la International Law Association, le Professeur *D. H. N. Johnson* de l'Université de Londres à écrit ainsi: "Moreover, as Prof. *H. Valladao* has pointed out in his paper published in 'The Freedom of the Air' (Edward McWhinney and M.A. Bradley, editors (1968)) and on other occasions, *the problem that has to be considered is definitely one of piracy. It is not correctly defined* by the newspaper definition of 'hi-jacking'. As our Chairman has explained, it is a question of a variety of forms of violence against aircraft, and such violence constitutes 'a new very serious crime, insofar as the violence against the aircraft will always and above all endanger the commander and the crew, or the passengers, who are abruptly and perilously obliged to land in a place which was not their destination'." Et le Prof. *Francisco P. Laplaza*, de l'Université de Buenos Aires, l'a appuyé catégoriquement; après avoir cité *Bynkdershoeck*, opinion déjà mentionée, il a déclaré: "My purpose is here to remember the classical Greek and Latin (*pirata; piraticum; piraticus*) roots of the word, common to every occidental language. The meaning is also clear to everybody more or less acquainted with semantic and with comparative law. On the contrary, 'hi-jacking' is not only a 'newspaper definition', that is to say, a common or vulgar definition, nor a technical one:

103

It is worse than that: it is a word taken from American cant, from the 'Lingo', from the language of the 'underworld'."

Dans le même sens, récemment, le Professeur *Evans* a affirmé: "On the other hand, 'hi-jacking', that relic of the Prohibition Era, is not entirely descriptive of the act, for in common usage hi-jacking applies to the seizure of a private commercial vehicle or vessel with the intent of theft of its load or cargo" (American Journal of International Law, Vol. 63 (1969) p. 696).

En réalité, une association scientifique, avec une aussi forte autorité que la presque centenaire "International Law Association" ne pourrait jamais briser une tradition doctrinaire remarquable et renommée, en employant une expression sans aucun caractère juridique, purement vulgaire, dans un sujet rigoureusement technique.

Plus encore, l'expression *légale*, employée dans les Codes et Lois pour les cas de capture violente de navires ou d'aéronefs, a toujours été, en France, *piraterie,* au Brésil (1830) et (1890), *pirateria*, en Italie, *pirateria*, dans les codes Hispanoaméricains, *pirateria*, et aux Etats Unis, *aircraft piracy*, selon ce que nous avons démontré auparavant, au n. 6. Et c'est aussi l'expression conventionnelle internationale, car la Convention de Genève, de 1958, déjà mentionnée, prévoit en utilisant le mot dans l'art. 15, la piraterie soit sur la mer, soit dans l'air, à bord d'un navire, ou d'un aéronef, aux fins d'effets juridictionnels en haute mer ou dans endroit non soumis à la souveraineté d'un Etat, et qui peut être même un *lieu où un aéronef est assailli à terre* (Prof. Laplaza). Quel est le motif pour abandonner, ainsi, le terme technico-juridique, légal et conventionnel, *piraterie*, de toutes les époques et de tous les lieux, en le remplaçant par un autre, d'emploi vulgaire, non-juridique, "hi-jacking"?

Finalement, il faut considérer que *le crime de piraterie*, est universellement connu par sa *très haute gravité* étant donné son caractère de super-banditisme, où il y a toujours la présence de la mort ou de la possibilité de la mort d'êtres humains innocents, utilisés comme otage d'une façon barbare. Il constitue assaut à main armée, violence inouïe, ou menance de violence contre des individus dans l'impossibilité de réagir ou de demander secours, par la surprise, la terreur et la lâcheté, avec laquelle il est pratiqué, surtout en des endroits dépourvus de police.

Il est inadmissible, ridicule même, de le considérer comme une simple délit de vol, appropriation ou détour illicite *d'une chose ou de son usage, ou de rendre plus difficile l'utilisation des moyens de transport, ou de simple restriction à la liberté individuelle de mouvements*—tous des délits sans cette gravité, punis par des peines bien inférieures.

On ne peut donc *jamais* leur concéder la catégorie de crime de piraterie, qui à cause de la forme, du lieu et des conséquences de sa pratique *constitue un délit contre l'humanité*, ses auteurs étant des assaillants terroristes, justement stigmatisés par la marque honteuse de "hostis humanis generis". Pour tout cela la piraterie est punie par les peines les plus sévères, elle est un crime de juridiction internationale quand elle est pratiquée en haute mer, dans l'air libre, ou dans un lieu hors de toute juridiction nationale et doit être un crime de punition internationale obligatoire.

Il serait ridicule d'établir la juridiction internationale pour un délit de "hi-jacking", de simple vol . . . l'illustre juriste pénal latino-américain, le Professeur *Sebastian Soler* l'a très bien dit: "Para alcanzar el concepto de pirataria se requiere un hecho de cierta magnitud por efecto de la cual pueda decirse que en realidad, no solamente ha sido afectado o puesto en peligro el derecho de propiedad, sino algun otro derecho" (Argentine Penal Law, IV, p. 580). Elle met en péril des biens inestimables, au-dessus d'Etats ou de Gouvernements, la vie, l'intégrité et la liberté des hommes, et la sûreté et la garantie de leur droit de communication (Vitoria).

L'importance du crime de piraterie et sa prolifération actuelle sur la mer et *surtout dans l'air, exigent sa punition internationale*, par tous les Etats, son élévation à une position au-dessus de la loi de chaque Etat, c'est-à-dire, à la catégorie de délit international, de "juris gentium", comme je l'ai soutenu depuis 1967 (H. Valladao, op. cit., pages 232/3) et dans des conférences réalisées dans des universités de l'Europe et des Amériques, en 1968 et 1969. Feu *H. Donnedieu des Vabres* a fait très bien voir que sa punition a pour but ". . . des valeurs immatérielles qui sont le patrimoine moral de l'humanité, et dont la destruction provoque un sentiment de réprobation universelle" (Principes de Droit Pénal International, p. 144).

Et l'unique moyen pour atteindre, efficacement ce but *est l'établissement multilatéral d'une convention internationale, par laquelle les Etats reconnaissent, formellement, le devoir de punir la piraterie, sur la mer ou dans l'air.*

Au sujet de ces délits internationaux il faut prendre pour base les conventions Internationales qui les ont prévus, des plus récentes, *l'Unique sur Stupéfiants*, de New York, 30/III/61 et celle de *Génocide* des Nations Unies, 9/XII/1948, aux plus anciennes, *Circulation et Trafic de Publications Obscènes*, Paris, 4/VIII/1910, et Genève, 12/IX/1923, *Trafic de Femmes et Enfants*, Paris, 4/V/1910, et Genève, 30/IX/1921, et *Destruction et Détérioration de Câbles Sous-Marins*, Paris, 14/III/1884, renouvelée par le Traité de Versailles, 28/VI/1919. *Il y a dans ces conventions plusieurs principes fondamentaux, qu'il faut utiliser maintenant.*

Le premier en est de proclamer le caractère international du crime, par ex. dans la Convention sur le *Génocide*, art. 1er, le deuxième — fondamental — est *l'affirmation du devoir de punir le crime pour les Etats*, en prenant dans leurs lois les mesures nécessaires, en imposant la prévision de ce crime et en donnant sa définition, et en exigeant l'imposition de punitions graves et efficaces, Stupéfiants, art. 36, I et II, *a*, Génocide, arts. II, III, IV et V, Publications Obscènes, art. 1er, Trafic de Femmes et Enfants, arts. I, II et III, Destruction et Détérioration de Câbles Sous-Marins, arts. II, V, VI et IX. Le troisième — très important — est de déclarer qu'il s'agit d'un crime *d'extradition obligatoire*, Stupéfiants, art. 36, 2, *b*, Génocide, art. VII (en ajoutant qu'il ne sera pas considéré crime politique pour ce but-là), Trafic de Femmes et Enfants, Paris, art. V (inclus de plein droit parmi les crimes qui autorisent l'extradition).

Les Etats qui ont ratifié ces conventions, comme le Brésil, ont inclu ces crimes tout de suite dans leurs Codes et Lois Pénales.

Dans le droit international coutumier la piraterie était considérée, sans rigueur technico-juridique comme un délit international.

Mais ce caractère sera développé en plusieurs conventions Internationales au sujet de la piraterie, au début bilatérales.

Ainsi dans le Traité d'Amitié, Commerce et Navigation, du 7 mars 1856 et du 12 octobre, en vigueur entre le Brésil et l'Argentine et l'Uruguai, dans l'article 13, les Etats *se promettent reciproquement de n'admettre aucuns pirates* dans leur ports et à les poursuivre par tous les moyens à leur disposition et *avec toute la rigueur des lois.*

De même dans les anciens Traités d'Extradition du Brésil, où les crimes étaient dénombrés (aujourd'hui ils sons prévus par le degré de la peine) la piraterie était toujours incluse. Ainsi le Traité avec l'Allemagne, art. I, n. 17, Belgique, art. III, n. 10, Grande Bretagne, art. II, n. 15, Espagne, art. III, n. 10: ("compris le fait de quelqu'un de s'emparer d'un navire à l'équipage duquel il appartient au moyen de fraude ou violence contre le commandant ou celui qui le remplace") Italie 12/XI/1872, art. III, 10 (identique à celui de l'Espagne, Pays-Bas, 21/XI/1895, art. I, n. 20 ("insubordination de passagers à bord d'un navire contre le commandant et de l'équipage contre ses supérieurs"), Paraguai, 16/I/1872, art. II, 13 ("y compris la capture par la tribulation"), Uruguai, 25/XI/1878, § 2e, n. 11 (*idem*). Et encore les textes de Conventions modernes, par ex. celle entre le Mexique et Cuba, du 25/V/1925, art. II, énumère parmi les délits possibles d'extradition, n. X, ceux pratiqués sur la mer, en spécifiant: "Comme la piraterie est connue et définie selon le droit international" (*H. Valladao*, op. cit., page 232). Ces clauses étaient communes aux Traités de l'époque, de la fin du XIXème et du début du XXème Siècle, comme on le voit dans ceux de l'Uruguai avec plusieurs pays de l'Amérique, Etats-Unis, art. II, 4 (inclusivement par la tribulation), et de l'Europe: Italie, Espagne, Suisse (*Julio Ma de Oarte*, Extradition, II, Montevideo, 1942); aussi dans ceux de Cuba, par ex. avec la Belgique, du 29/X/1904, où on peut lire, se rapportant à la marine marchande dans l'art. II, n. 8: "Pirateria o revolucion a bordo de buques cuando la tripulacion o los pasageros se apoderen del buque por sorpresa o violencia contra el capitan" (*Bustamante*, Manual de Derecho Internacional Privado, Havana, 1941, 2nd edition, p. 417).

Est prévue, aussi dans des actes internationaux, la forme

actuelle de piraterie, des navires ou bateaux *Santa Maria, Jack Rogers, Columbia Eagle, ou des avions.*

Parmi les traités plurilatéraux, que nous avons déjà cités (n. 6), la Convention Pan-Américaine de la Havane (*Code Bustamante*), de 1928, ratifiée par quinze Etats américains, inclut dans l'art 308, la Piraterie dans le régime général des Délits Internationaux, à côté du trafic de nègres et du commerce d'esclaves, le trafic de femmes, la destruction ou la détérioration des câbles sous-marins et des autres délits du même caractère *commis en haute mer, à l'air libre et dans des territoires non organisés encore sous la forme d'Etats.* Le Traité de Droit Pénal International de Montevideo, ratifié par plusieurs Etats Américains en particulier par l'Uruguay et l'Argentine, art. 14, en maintenant le même principe, a cependant, concédé *le droit de préférence, à l'Etat où les délits ont été accomplis,* de solliciter par la voie de l'extradition la livraison des délinquants.

Il faut noter que le Traité n'a pas fait pour ces crimes la réserve, *habituelle dans les Traités d'Extradition de ces Etats,* des crimes politiques, des crimes communs connexes avec des crimes politiques ou avec des buts politiques.

Cela s'explique, l'offense à un bien juridique de caractère humain universel, caractéristique ces crimes "de juris gentium", étant supérieure à tout intérêt de nature individuelle.

Finalement, selon ce que nous avons vu au n. 5, la Convention de Genève, 1958, quoique punissant la piraterie aussi dans les airs en ce qui concerne les aéronefs, l'a définie avec un *manque d'actualisation incompréhensible,* seulement dans le cas d'un acte pratiqué *par un navire* ou aéronef contre un *autre* navire ou aéronef, divergeant même du Projet à ce sujet de l'ancienne commission d'Experts de la Société des Nations, de 1926, art. 1er: "commettre sur la mer libre à son propre compte, des actes qui impliquent pillage de biens ou actes de violence contre personnes."

Devant ce que nous avons exposé, l'actualisation urgente du droit de la piraterie, sur la mer et dans l'air s'impose; selon ce que nous avons soutenu cela est possible en établissant entre tous les Etats une convention Internationale sur la Punition de la Piraterie, maritime et aérienne.

Les Nations Unies se sont manifestées, récemment, dans ce

sens à travers la Résolution du 12/XII/1969, *mais sans précision technico-juridique, en parlant du détournement par la force d'aéronefs civils en vol.*

L'idée a été soutenue aussi, avant d'être adoptée par les Nations Unies, par le Professeur *Evans*, qui écrivait: "But as aircraft hi-jacking is essentially an international criminal offence, the need is for concerted action by States at this level, that is, a commitment to recognize the seriousness of the offence, to adopt punitive legislation to the offence and to agree to the extradition of hi-jackers." (The American Journal of International Law, Vol. 63, p. 707).

Peu importe ce que disent certains pessimistes, déclarant, comme toujours, désirer le maximum mais empêchant toute réalisation considérable, lorsqu'ils affirment que la convention ne serait ni signée, ni ratifiée par certains Etats. . .

La même chose arriva, d'abord, avec d'autres conventions qui punissaient des délits internationaux, par ex., celle de stupéfiants, mais, à la fin, les Etats récalcitrants ont adhéré, devant la grande force de l'opinion publique en faveur de la répression de ces crimes infâmes.

La Convention projetée sera différente de la Convention de Genève de 1958, sur la Haute Mer, qui a traité du sujet, selon ce que nous avons vu, d'une façon précaire, incomplète et non actuelle.

Le nouvel acte international prévu maintenant est *plus* ample et sera *même complet.*

Voyons les bases de la nouvelle convention. Elle va contraindre les Etats, dans son art. 1er, à punir le crime de piraterie comme un délit "juris gentium", c'est-à-dire: I) à inclure dans leurs lois la punition de la piraterie maritime et aérienne, en prévoyant et précisant le crime respectif et le menaçant de peines sévères et efficaces, et II) à instruire un procès et juger respectivement les auteurs, co-auteurs et complices, lorsqu'un de ceux-là tombe sous leur juridiction, *quelque soit le lieu où le crime aura été pratiqué,* sauf l'extradition prévue dans l'article 4. Ayant formulé ce principe de base, la convention va le consolider dans l'article suivant, 2, lui donnant non seulement une éfficacité réelle (qui est le fait de l'art. 1er — le précepte traditionnel du droit coutumier, en termes facultatifs, reproduit dans l'art. 19 de la convention de Genève) mais un caractère impératif: obligeant tout état à capturer en haute mer, dans l'air libre, ou dans n'importe quel lieu non soumis à la juridiction d'un état, un navire ou aéronef quelconque où des actes de piraterie sont en train d'être pratiqués.

Dans l'article 3 de la convention prévue le crime de piraterie serait défini *par un assaut pratiqué à l'aide ou à bord d'un navire actualisant* la définition très limitée de l'art. 15 pour inclure la dernière forme de piraterie maritime et aérienne, qui prolifère depuis 1961, avec les cas des captures du navire *Santa Maria*, conduit de Caracas à Recife, et de l'avion des Etats-Unis, détourné du Mexique pour Cuba.

Dans ce but *seraient considérées les définitions* données pour les cas similaires dans les anciens codes et lois, déjà cités de la France, d'Italie, d'Espagne, du Brésil et de plusieurs états latino-américaines et de Traités, aussi cités à propos d'extradition.

Et aussi les nouvelles dispositions législatives, peu après ces faits, des Etats-Unis, Aircraft Piracy, et, récemment, de l'Argentine et du Mexique, en 1968 et de Cuba, en 1969.

En conformité avec cela, sauf formulation meilleure, l'article 3, devrait déclarer: "Le crime de piraterie est commis par: 1) quiconque capture illicitement un navire privé ou un aéronef privé ou en prend le contrôle, ou essaye de pratiquer de tels actes, au moyen de violence, menace de violence, surprise, actes de terrorisme, fraude ou d'autres méthodes;
2) quiconque pratique illicitement, pour des fins personnelles des actes de violence, de détention ou de n'importe quel pillage, à l'aide d'un navire ou aéronef privé contre un autre navire ou aéronef ou contre des personnes ou biens à bord de ce navire ou aéronef; 3) quiconque incite ou aide, directement ou indirectement, la pratique des crimes prévus aux numéros antérieurs".

Il faut noter que la définition du crime de piraterie maritime ou aérienne a été donnée d'une façon générique, *indépendemment du lieu où se trouve le navire ou l'aéronef*, parce qu'il s'agit de la définition d'un délit international, "juris gentium", qui *doit être* puni n'importe où il aura été *commis*. Et *peu importe que le navire ou l'avion soit en mouvement ou à l'arrêt*.

Peu importe, aussi, pour les autres délits internationaux, que le génocide, que le commerce ou l'action de faciliter l'utilisation de stupéfiants, que le trafic de femmes et enfants, etc.—soient pratiqués nationalement ou internationalement, dans un état ou en haute mer ou dans l'air libre ou dans un territoire hors de la juridiction d'un état.

Punir la piraterie maritime ou aérienne intéresse toute l'humanité, même lorsqu'elle est pratiqués en eaux ou espaces territoriaux, ou dans le territoire d'un état.

C'était dans ce but qu'on a crée le délit international, ayant en vue de ne laisser jamais impuni un crime ainsi infâme.

Ensuite, dans un article 4, il serait établi que: "Chaque état accordera, selon ses lois et traités, l'extradition des criminels sollicités par l'état dans le territoire duquel le crime a été réalisé, ainsi considéré celui de la capture d'un navire ou d'un aéronef, ou du contrôle d'un navire ou d'un aéronef, ou celui de la réalisation des actes qui constituent une tentative", en ajoutant dans une deuxième alinéa que si un tel crime était "réalisé en haute mer, dans l'air libre ou territoire de la juridiction d'aucun état, l'extradition serait accordée à l'état de la nationalité du navire ou de l'inscription de l'aéronef".

Les mots "selon ses lois et traités" autorisent certaines exceptions admises par le droit interne, comme celle qui oblige l'état qui sollicite l'extradition à ne pas appliquer certaines peines comme celle de mort.

La Résolution des Nations Unies du 12/12/69 n'a pas considéré les principes courants ci-dessus en ce qui concerne les délits internationaux et leur punition.

Elle a limité le crime seulement aux actes pratiqués dans des aéronefs en vol (titre de la Résolution et conclusion 7, bien qu'au numéro 3 on parle, d'une façon générique, de la capture d'un aéronef civil) ce qui est inadmissible parce que la capture ou la tentative de capture d'un navire ou d'un aéronef, ni navigant ni volant, *est possible et est déjà arrivée.*

Etant donné le haut intérêt du trafic maritime ou aérien et le péril généralisé qui en découle, le fait ne constitue pas un simple larcin ou vol mais un délit très grave dans le cadre des délits internationaux.

Le projet de Convention du Comité Légal de l'Organisation

Internationale de l'Aviation Civile aussi n'a pas considéré les principes fonamentaux en ce qui concerne la punition de délits internationaux.

En limitant à "any person who on board an aircraft in flight . . .", le projet s'est limité non seulement au cas d'un aéronef *en vol*, mais aussi aux personnes, auteurs ou autres participants, qui sont à bord de l'aéronef alors que les co-auteurs ou complices, à la punition desquels le projet prévoit aussi (art. 1er, *b*), peuvent étre à terre.

D'ailleurs des textes au sujet de piraterie maritime prévoient la punition des complices, à terre, des pirates.

D'autre part l'article 2, n. 3 et 4, plus restrictif que la convention des Nations Unies, le limite à des vols internationaux, exclut du contenu de la Convention le crime pratiqué dans le territoire de l'état où l'aéronef est enregistré, ce qui est incompatible et est même en contradiction avec toutes les conventions internationales, déjà citées plusieurs fois, qui établissant l'obligation de punir des délits internationaux, y incluent toujours les délits pratiqués dans le territoire des états contractants.

Aussi dans l'article 4 du Projet du Comité Légal on ne reconnait pas, comme il est courant dans la matière, à l'état qui capture les coupables la compétence pour le procès et le jugement du crime (sauf l'extradition. en faveur de l'état ou le crime a été commis).

Il faut noter encore que le Projet ne donne pas de titre au crime, *le considérant innommé*, se limitant dans sa définition à déclarer "commits an offence herein after referred to as 'the offence' ".

L'article 4 de notre Convention proposée devrait stipuler: "Chaque état devrait assurer, selon ses lois, l'extradition de criminels demandée par l'état dans le territoire duquel le crime a été commis, ou l'éxécution des actes constitutifs de la tentative a eu lieu", en ajoutant dans un autre paragraphe: "Dans le cas d'un crime commis en haute mer, dans l'air libre ou dans un lieu non soumis à la juridiction d'aucun état, l'extradition sera assurée à l'Etat de la nationalité du navire ou à l'Etat où l'aéronef a été enregistré".

Finalement, dans l'article 5, il serait disposé que: "Les

112

crimes prévus dans l'article 3 ne constituent pas des crimes politiques ni peuvent être considérés pratiqués avec des buts politiques, soit pour autoriser la concession d'asile territorial ou diplomatique, soit pour dénier une demande d'extradition".

Nous avons déjà vu qu'un délit international contre l'humanité serait un non-sens, s'il pourrait être qualifié, par un état quelconque, de crime politique ou de crime pratiqué avec des buts politiques.

Dans ce sens nous avons déjà montré ce que la convention sur le génocide a disposé expressément dans son article 3 et, au Brésil, l'article 6 de la Loi 28689, du 1/X/1956, qui en accomplissant la Convention, a puni et défini le crime de génocide.

Récemment, selon la presse (Brésil, *Jornal do Brasil*, 22/XI/69 et *Jornal do Comércio*, 5/XII/69) les Etats-Unis étaient en train de négocier avec l'Espagne et, ensuite, avec la France, l'inclusion dans les traités d'extradition respectifs, soit des pirates aériens, soit des contrebandiers de drogues, et avec la Grande Bretagne un nouveau Traité d'Extradition, comprenant les pirates de l'air.

En conférence au PEN Club du Brésil, à Rio de Janeiro, le 1er décembre 1969, nous avons démontré que: "Le problème de l'extradition pour les crimes de piraterie aérienne doit être examiné de nouveau en ce qui concerne l'ancien principe de la non-extradition pour les délits politiques. Déjà quand ce principe a été créé, les lois et conventions ont prévu que ne s'applique pas d'exception aux crimes internationaux, par exemple d'anarchisme ou terrorisme. Evidemment, dans un conflit entre l'intérêt général de l'humanité et l'asile politique, le premier doit surpasser le second." (*Jornal do Brasil* 2/XII/69).

J'ai fait référence au Traité d'Extradition et Protection contre l'Anarchisme, du Mexique, le 28/I/1902, dans l'article 2 duquel après avoir établi l'absence d'extradition pour délits politiques, on a ajouté: "Will not be reputed as political offence acts considered as anarchism by the laws of the solicitant States and the one which receives the request." Ainsi l'a établi aussi le grand juriste brésilien, *Epitacio Pessoa*, ancien Juge de la Cour de la Haye, dans le Projet de Code Panaméricain de Droit International Public, art. 228, § 2e. Dans le même sens, l'Institut de Droit International, dans sa session de Genève, du 8/IX/1892, Art. 4: "Ne sont point réputés délits politiques les faits délictueux qui sont dirigés contre les bases de toute organisation sociale, et non pas seulement contre tel état déterminé ou contre telle forme de gouvernment". (Résolution de 8/9/1922).

J'ai montré, encore, que la 6ème Conférence Internationale pour l'Unification du Droit Pénal, réalisée à Copenhague le 31/VIII/1935, en précisant les Délits Politiques, a déclaré: "Will not be considered political infringements those which create a common danger or a state of terror".

Aussi le Comité Juridique Interaméricain de Rio de Janeiro, dans une étude le 4/11/1959 sur le même sujet, avait déclaré que: "No son delitos politicos los crimenes de barbarie y vandalismo, y en general todas las infracciones que exceden esos limites licitos del ataque y la defensa." (4) "No es delito politico el genocidio, de acuerdo con la convencion de las Naciones Unidas."

Il serait vraiment incompréhensible que l'auteur d'un délit international obtienne l'asile ou la dénégation de la demande de son extradition, en alléguant que la détérioration ou destruction d'un câble sous-marin, le trafic de femmes ou enfants, le commerce ou l'action visant à faciliter l'utilisation de stupéfiants, le génocide, la piraterie, le terrorisme sont des crimes politiques ... ou qu'il les aurait pratiqués avec des buts politiques ...; dernièrement, parmi les crimes de terrorisme on trouve aussi le crime de commerce et utilisation de stupéfiants.

D'ailleurs la dénégation de l'asile aux pirates est traditionnelle. Nous l'avons déjà noté, avant (n. 11), dans le Traité Brésil-Argentine de 1856, et *Dudley Field* l'a consolidé dans l'article 84 de son Projet de Code de Droit International: *"Interdiction de donner asile à des pirates",* 84 —"Aucune nation ne peut recevoir des pirates dans son territoire ou permettre que quelqu'un les y reçoive, protège, recèle ou assiste d'une manière quelconque: elle doit punir tous ceux qui se rendent coupables de tels actes." (Projet, Trad. française) (1884).

Il faut rappeler, enfin que la Convention Internationale pour la Prévention et Répression du Terrorisme, patronnée par l'ancienne Société des Nations, a considéré comme délit de terrorisme, art. II, n. 3: "El hecho intencional que pone en riesgo vidas humanas por la creacion de un peligro commun" et accordait expressément, Art. VIII, n. 3 l'extradition due.

Et elle créait, aussi—ce qui me parait très raisonnable—une Cour Criminelle Internationale pour le jugement des accusés, dans le cas où l'état le préfère, au lieu d'accorder l'extradition.

Le Projet de Convention signé à la Haye le 16 décembre 1970 est très faible du point de vue technique et juridique.

D'abord, il s'appelle "Convention pour la Suppression de l'Appropriation Illégale de l'Aéronef"... Une Convention ne peut pas décréter la suppression d'un crime.

D'autre part, il n'a pas suivi le bon chemin des autres conventions pour la punition de délits internationaux, très connues et déjà citées.

Il ne donne pas au moins un nom pour le délit: il dit article 1 *fine*, qu'il s'appelle simplement "délit" (*"offence"*)...

Elle ne s'applique pas, art. 3. ns. 3 et 4, aux délits *réalisés intégralement dans le territoire de l'état du registre,* même si l'avion est en voyage international, ce qui contredit toutes les conventions sur les délits internationaux et laisse sans protection les passagers, même internationaux, qui voyagent dans un avion détourné dans et pour le pays de son registre.

Et le danger et le crime sont les mêmes... Et alors vient l'exception contradictoire du n. 5 de l'article 3.

Elle ne punit pas l'appropriation réalisée lorsque l'appareil n'est pas en vol, art. 1^0, ce qui—nous avons vu—est possible et dangereux.

Elle ne dit pas de manière expresse que le crime est un crime commun, laissant ouvert tout le problème du motif politique... même si le délit est de terrorisme.

La complicité, art. 1, *b*, et l'extradition, art. 8, ont été bien prévues selon ce que j'ai défendu dans mes travaux cités, et au-dessus, numéros 15 et 16.

Chapter 7

HIJACKING, INTERNATIONAL LAW AND HUMAN
RIGHTS

by Oliver J. Lissitzyn

It is not necessary to retrace all the events that have led to the
mounting concern of the world community with unlawful
seizure of aircraft (which for the sake of simplicity, we will
call "hijacking") and all the efforts to deal with it; nor is it
necessary to engage in close textual critique of every provision
in the various existing and proposed treaties and resolutions
addressed to the matter. Rather, we will look to the substance
of some of these provisions and also to some problems that
must be faced.

In simplest and broadest terms, the provisions and proposals
with which we are concerned have two major objectives. The
first objective is to assure the safety and the speedy return or
release, as may be appropriate, of the hijacked passengers,
crews, cargoes and aircraft. The second objective is to prevent
hijacking, through deterrence or otherwise.

To accomplish the first objective, the Tokyo Convention of
1963 on Offences and Certain Other Acts Committed on
Board Aircraft provides in its Article 11:

"1. When a person on board has unlawfully committed by force or threat
thereof an act of interference, seizure, or other wrongful exercise of
control of an aircraft in flight or when such an act is about to be committed, Contracting States shall take all appropriate measure to restore control of the aircraft to its lawful commander or to preserve his control of
the aircraft.
2. In the cases contemplated in the preceding paragraph, the Contracting
State in which the aircraft lands shall permit its passengers and crew to
continue their journey as soon as practicable, and shall return the aircraft
and its cargo to the persons lawfully entitled to possession."

116

This is the only provision of its kind that is already formally in force for a number of states. Substantially similar, but even briefer, is Article 9 of the Draft Convention on Unlawful Seizure of Aircraft prepared by the Legal Committee of the International Civil Aviation Organization (ICAO) in March 1970.

The Assembly of ICAO, in Resolutions A17-5 and A17-8, adopted at its Seventeenth (Extraordinary) Session in June 1970, recommended and urged, in some detail, measures "to alleviate the consequences of unlawful seizure," including the return of aircraft and cargo "to the persons lawfully entitled to possession," permission for the passengers and crews to continue their journeys "as soon as practicable," and "measures for the safety and care of passengers and crew . . . until their journey can be continued." And on 9 September 1970 the Security Council of the United Nations, in its Resolution 286 (1970), appealed "to all parties concerned for the immediate release of all passengers and crews without exception, held as a result of hijackings and other interference in international travel."

There is grave danger, however, in such hortatory language and in regarding the obligation of return or release as arising only from treaty provisions such as Article 11 of the Tokyo Convention. Few, if any, multilateral treaties are universally ratified. The Tokyo Convention, seven years after its formulation in 1963, had been ratified or acceded to by only thirty states. I submit that the duty to return hijacked aircraft and cargoes and to release their passengers and crews without unjustified delay is already established in general international law by custom and is binding on all states. It is evidenced by such return and release in the overwhelming majority of actual instances of hijacking. In some cases, moreover, such action has been accompanied by statements to the effect that it is required by international practice. On the other hand, few, if any, states have claimed a general right to detain hijacked aircraft and their occupants. Furthermore, no legitimate interest can be adversely affected by denying the existence of such a right. We would be amply justified, therefore, in affirming the rule of return and release as one already established and binding on all states regardless of treaty obligations. Treaty provisions on this point should be cast in declaratory terms. There should also be declaratory resolutions unequivocally affirming the rule. Such resolutions should be adopted by the most authoritative and widely representative international organs—preferably by both the Assembly of ICAO and the General Assembly of the United Nations.

Furthermore, well-established rules of state responsibility in customary international law require states to use due diligence to protect the persons and property of foreign nationals within their territories from harm, and to take effective measures to prosecute and punish individuals who commit crimes against foreign nationals. These duties must be regarded as particularly exacting when the foreigners are present within the state's territory by compulsion rather than by choice.

A corollary of the duty of prompt return and release is the recognition of certain immunities or exemptions from local jurisdiction for foreign aircraft and their occupants entering in distress, by analogy with the immunity of foreign ships in distress. The rationale of immunity of vessels in distress certainly applies to aircraft, and the principle of immunity should be stated accordingly. Aircraft in distress include, of course, those arriving under the control of hijackers. A degree of immunity has, in fact, been granted to hijacked foreign aircraft and their occupants in a large majority of cases. Passengers and crew members, for example, are generally not penalized for attempted entry without required documents such as visas and are not compelled to pay customs duties on articles they have with them. But the immunity extends further and includes freedom from prosecution for past offenses. If such immunity is not recognized, some states might be tempted to take advantage of a hijacking—and perhaps even to procure one—to detain or prosecute some passengers for alleged political or other crimes which have no connection with the hijacking or with any events aboard the aircraft during the flight.

The rules of general international law I have just stated are not intended to prevent a state in which a hijacked aircraft lands from conducting an investigation of reasonable scope and duration, including search of the aircraft and its occupants, if there is ground for suspecting that the entry was not really in distress and that it threatens the security of the state of landing.

Much more complex and difficult is the problem of deterring and thus preventing hijacking through international agreement. Important as this objective is, it cannot be regarded as an absolute which overrides all other considerations and values.

Suppose that a group of victims of Nazi persecutions in Germany had hijacked a German plane and escaped to a democracy. The objective of deterrence of hijacking would have been best served by returning them to Hitler's mercies. But should this have been enough to convince the adherents of justice and humanity—in short, of what we now call human rights—to agree to do it? My answer is, *No!* Revulsion against the recent series of hijackings must not blind us to the force of other considerations. Foremost among these must be respect for human rights—respect to which most governments pay at least lip service.

In order to give due weight to the considerations that must be taken into account, we must distinguish between the different purposes that hijacking can serve. At one end of the scale, are hijackings committed deliberately for the purpose of inflicting harm on innocent passengers—as by holding them as hostages—or destroying the aircraft. This is the kind of hijackings that have recently shocked world opinion and intensified the search for an international solution of the problem. In dealing with such hijackings—which are themselves gross violations of human rights—the objective of prevention through deterrence must be given very great weight. At the other end of the scale are hijackers trying to escape from countries whose governments deny or disregard human rights and do not permit their citizens or subjects, with very few exceptions, to leave the country by normal, lawful means. The existence of such governments, unfortunately, is not a myth but an all-too-evident reality. (It is indeed possible that their number will increase.) In these circumstances, hijacking may even appear to be the only effective means of asserting and protecting human rights, as in the example of people escaping from Hitler. Between these extremes, there is a spectrum of

119

possible purposes. Ordinary criminals may be fleeing from justice. In many cases, hijacked aircraft are used simply as convenient means of transportation without the costs and the formalities of lawful travel, or of gaining entry into a country which might otherwise not permit it. Deplorable as all such hijackings are, it is well to keep in mind that hijackings simply for the purpose of travel have caused, despite their frequency, very few injuries to persons and very few cases of damage to aircraft. The resolution (LXXI-6) adopted by the Council of ICAO on 1 October 1970 properly recognizes the significance of the purpose of a hijacking:

"THE COUNCIL,

FINDING that a heightened threat to the safety and security of international civil air transport exists as a result of acts of unlawful seizure of aircraft involving the detention of passengers, crew and aircraft contrary to the principles of Article 11 of the Tokyo Convention, for international blackmail purposes, and the destruction of such aircraft;
. . .

CALLS upon Contracting States, in order to ensure the safety and security of international civil air transport, upon request of a Contracting State to consult together immediately with a view to deciding what joint action should be undertaken, in accordance with international law, without excluding measures such as the suspension of international civil air transport services to and from any State which after the unlawful seizure of an aircraft, detains passengers crew or aircraft contrary to the principles of Article 11, for international blackmail purposes, or any State which, contrary to the principles of Articles 7 and 8 of the Draft Convention on Unlawful Seizure of Aircraft, fails to extradite or prosecute persons committing acts of unlawful seizure for international blackmail purposes; . . ."

The term "international blackmail" is not defined, but apparently means the holding of passengers, crews and aircraft as hostages to exact compliance with the hijackers' demands. The Council of ICAO thus indicates that hijacking for this purpose is a particularly serious offense, and that states which cooperate with it deserve particularly severe sanctions.

There are, indeed, two major means of deterring hijackings by international agreement. One is extradition. The other is punishment by states in which the hijackers are apprehended. As you may have already gathered, I would not regard as desirable a general multilateral agreement providing for the

120

extradition of all hijackers without exception to the country of registration of the aircraft or to the country in which the hijackers first boarded the aircraft. There may be circumstances in which such extradition would be violative of the basic values of human rights. I am in favor, therefore, of the solution proposed in the Draft Convention prepared by ICAO's Legal Committee:

"Article 8
1. The offence shall be deemed to be included as an extraditable offence in any extradition treaty existing between Contracting States. Contracting States undertake to include the offence as an extraditable offence in every extradition treaty to be concluded between them.
2. The Contracting States which do not make extradition conditional on the existence of a treaty shall recognize the offence as an extraditable offence between themselves subject to the conditions established by the law of the State requested to extradite.
3. The offence shall be treated, for the purpose of extradition between Contracting States, as if it had been committed not only in the place in which it occurred but also in the territory:
(a) of the State of registration of the aircraft;
(b) of every State in which the aircraft lands with the alleged offender still on board."

This provision would not compel states to enter into new extradition treaties or to regard as inapplicable, in cases of hijacking, the traditional exception, contained in most extradition treaties, of political offenses. This exception is itself in part an early reflection on the international plane of concern for human rights, as is the non-existence of a general international duty of extradition. Indeed, a convention that contained an iron-clad, general provision for automatic extradition of all hijackers without exception would not be likely to gain general acceptance within the international community.

I am quite aware of the argument that all hijackings endanger the lives of passengers and crew members, and therefore impinge on human rights; and that, therefore, the objective of deterrence, which is best served by a general obligation of automatic extradition, must be given more weight than the protection of the human rights of hijackers. However, in the light of the fact that hijackings for the purpose of travel have caused very few actual injuries, I am not convinced by

121

this argument. I must concede, however, that the weighing of the values involved is necessarily a subjective decision, as is the weighing of all ultimate values. There is no objective criterion that can be applied.

A substantial measure of deterrence can be provided by a general multilateral agreement imposing on the states in which alleged hijackers land the obligation to take them into custody and if they are not extradited to try them in the courts of those states — assuming, of course, that such an agreement is very widely, if not universally, ratified. The duty to take an alleged offender into custody is stated in Article 6, paragraph 1, of the Draft Convention prepared by the Legal Committee of ICAO. Article 7, furthermore, provides:

"The Contracting State which has taken measures pursuant to Article 6, paragraph 1, shall, if it does not extradite the alleged offender, be obliged to submit the case to its competent authorities for their decision whether to prosecute him. These authorities shall take their decision in the same manner as in the case of other offences."

I agree with Mr. Butler that the obligation to prosecute should be stated in stronger terms, but I foresee technical as well as political difficulties in drafting such terms.

Article 3 of the Draft Convention provides: "Each Contracting State undertakes to make the offence punishable by severe penalties." I agree with the failure of this clause to define "severe." A court, in imposing the sentence, should be free to consider much factors as the purpose, motivation, and the actual consequances of the offense. The "severity" of a penalty is relative to all the relevant factors. No one has the right to hijack aircraft, and all hijackers should be punished, but not all should be punished equally.

Ideally, the proper weighing of all the relevant considerations could perhaps be best accomplished by a special international tribunal with a world-wide base, as recently suggested by the Secretary-General of the United Nations, but the chances of such a tribunal being established in the foreseeable future are practically nil. Perhaps less improbable might be the establishment of an international or joint tribunal for this purpose by a group of like-minded states, but even this step is likely to encounter great difficulties, both political and technical. Nevertheless, its feasibility deserves further exploration. If no such tribunal is established, the adequacy of sentences imposed by national courts in cases of aggravated hijacking—such as that for "international blackmail" purposes—could be roughly appraised by the international community if provision were made for effective sanctions against states whose courts failed to impose adequate sentences. Effective sanctions would include the interruption of international air transport relations with the offending states, as rather tentatively mentioned in the resolution of the Council of ICAO adopted on 1 October 1970 and in part reproduced above. I hope that such a sanction could be included in any further Convention on the problem of hijacking.

The chances of hijackers being punished would be further enhanced, if only modestly, by a provision permitting *all* states to exercise criminal jurisdiction over alleged hijackers apprehended within their territory, regardless of the place of commission of the offense, the state of registration of the hijacked aircraft, or the nationality of the offenders or their victims. Such a provision would make the offense of hijacking resemble more closely the traditional crime of piracy on the high seas than it does now.

One problem that has to be faced, with any international Convention on hijacking, is that of the permissibility of reservations. Unless it be provided that no reservations may be attached to the ratifications and accessions to the Convention, the practical value of the Convention is likely to be further diluted.

In conclusion, I must confess that I remain rather skeptical of the chances of any really adequate convention being so widely adopted by states as to be a truly effective solution of the problem of hijacking. Pending such adoption, every government interested in the prevention of hijacking must devise and implement effective security measures at its airports and on its aircraft. It must also use all the influence at its disposal to enhance the probability of all hijackers being adequately punished, with due regard to the basic values of human rights, as well as to assure the safety and well-being of the victims of this grave offense.

Chapter 8

HIJACKING AND THE RIGHT OF ASYLUM

by L.C. Green

According to Article 14 of the Universal Declaration of Human Rights, adopted by the General Assembly of the United Nations on December 10, 1948, "everyone has the right to seek and enjoy in other countries asylum from persecution". This right, however, is not as unlimited as might appear at first sight. In the first place, there is no concomitant duty placed upon any state to confer upon the asylum seeker that which he seeks. Second, the Article itself provides that "this right may not be invoked in the case of prosecutions genuinely arising from non-political crimes or from acts contrary to the purposes and principles of the United Nations". Moreover, the Declaration is nothing more than a General Assembly Resolution which lacks binding force and may be considered as little more than a pious statement of aims to be achieved. As if to reiterate this fact, the International Covenant on Civil and Political Rights, which was opened for signature on December 19, 1966, and by the end of 1969 had received only 6 of the required 35 ratifications to bring it into force, makes no reference whatever to this *soi-disant* right. However, presumably by way of what might be considered a sop to the world, on December 14, 1967, the General Assembly unanimously adopted the Declaration on Asylum. This merely asserts that if, acting within its sovereign rights, a state grants asylum to a person invoking Article 14 of the Universal Declaration, that asylum shall be respected by all other states, and "it shall rest with the state granting asylum to evaluate the grounds for the grant of asylum". This Declaration is no more substantive than the Universal Declaration. Furthermore, it makes it clear that whatever right the asylum seeker may assert he is entitled to, it will be for the state to which he applies to decide solely within its own discretion whether grounds exist for the claim to be made, while there is still no duty to grant the asylum even though it is found that good grounds exist.

It is clear from Article 14 that there are two types of political fugitive. On the one hand there are those who flee a county merely because they actually or purportedly disagree with the local political system or regime, and whose reception depends entirely on the political discretion of the receiving state — which often means on the prevailing state of relations between the country of flight and that of reception. Second, there are those who are alleged by the state of flight to have committed some offence, but who contend that the acts of which they are accused are politically motivated, sufficiently so to render them exempt from extradition processes, and who maintain that if they are not granted asylum by the state to which they have come, then they should not be subjected to *refoulement* either. In the case of aerial hijackers, there is, always, even when the escape has been solely for political reasons, some crime attached to the act, be it kidnapping of passengers and crew, endangering the aircraft, unlawful detention of government property, or something of that kind. There is no possibility for the fugitive to maintain that he is nothing but a political refugee who is completely free of any criminal charge. This makes it necessary to consider the nature of political offences as recognised in international practice and to assess the extent to which aerial hijackers may contend that they fall within this classification.

Broadly speaking, it may be stated that the whole basis of the concept of the political offence is that the offender is wanted in respect of acts committed by him against the government seeking his recovery and punishment. The starting point for this view of the matter, at least in so far as judicial practive is concerned, is *Re Castioni*[1] an English decision which seems to have received general support. Denman J. laid down that for an offence to be considered political, "it must

---

[1] [1891] 1 Q.B. 149, 156, 159.

at least be shown that the act is done in furtherance of, done with the intention of assistance, as a sort of overt act in the course of acting in a political manner, a political rising, or a dispute between two parties in the State as to which is to have the government in its hands. ... The question really is, whether, upon the facts, it is clear that the man was acting as one of a number of persons engaged in acts of violence of a political character with a political object, and as part of the political movement and rising in which he was taking part." Such a definition would clearly not extend to a private act taken by a single individual either for his own political ends, or because he was politically opposed to the country in which his offence was alleged to have been committed.

Many of the hijackers of recent times have described themselves as anarchists, even though they may have sought asylum, or asserted that it was their intention to seek such asylum, within a country that subscribed to a political philosophy other than that of anarchism, whatever that may mean when applied to a governmental system, unless it be that of the anarcho-syndicalists of the former Spanish Republic. Shortly after *Castioni*, an English judge made it clear that anarchists could never claim political asylum. In *Re Meunier*[2] Cave J. stated that "to constitute an offence of a political character, there must be two or more parties in the State, each seeking to impose the Government of their own choice on the other, and that, if the offence is committed by one side or the other in pursuance of that object, it is a political offence, otherwise not. In the present case there are not two parties in the State, each seeking to impose the Government of their own choice on the other; for the party with whom the accused is identified . . ., namely, the party of anarchy, is the enemy of all Governments."

This attitude to anarchists was applied generally by the European powers. In 1894 France returned Livourne to Italy for the murder of the journalist Bandi, killed in the name of anarchist vengeance. Similarly, in 1901 Switzerland returned to Italy the anarchist Jaffei wanted in connection with the

[2] [1894] 2 Q.B. 415, 419.

126

assassination of Umberto I. Some countries have carried the denial of the political character to anarchists to an extent that even embraces communists. Thus, Article 153 of the 1950 Constitution of El Salvador guaranteed asylum to aliens and forbade their extradition for political offences, while Article 20 took the right of residence away from aliens "who promulgate anarchical or undemocratic doctrines." Some Latin American countries have embodied this principle in their treaty practice and the Brazilian-Bolivian Treaty of 1938 stipulates that "criminal acts which constitute an open manifestation of anarchy, or are designed to overthrow the bases of all social organisation shall not be considered as political offences." This is in line with the Pan-American Convention for the Extradition of Criminals and for Protection against Anarchism, 1902, providing that "extradition shall not be granted for political offences or for deeds connected therewith. There shall not be considered as political offences acts which may be classified as pertaining to anarchism, by the legislation of both the demanding country and the country from whom the demand is made." The Central American Extradition Convention of 1934 not only denies a political character to anarchistic acts, but also to "attempts against the life of the head of a government or public functionaries"—a matter which is of increasing importance in view of the present "popularity" of kidnappings affecting political personalities and foreign diplomats.

The position here described is based on the nineteenth century concept of liberal democracy with an organised party system, where normally there would be two parties struggling for supremacy and violence would not be considered the most normal way changing from one party to another. Nor was it considered normal that a change of party would result in a change in the political or governmental system and those who were committed to a clear rejection of the then-accepted system were frequently denied political asylum. Thus in the *Malatesta* case, 1891, the Swiss Federal Court pointed out that the association with which the accused was connected sought "the overthrow of the established political and social order, and its replacement by another political and economic system, namely anarchism. While it was true that there was a clearly political end, the means by which this was sought was not so much peaceful propaganda as by the use of violence, directed to overthrowing the existing political system and redistributing the economic wealth. Such an aim involves offences against persons and property. Such an association is in reality not a political organisation, but a band of thieves or brigands."[3]

This view comes very close to the decision of Mathers C.J. of the Manitoba King's Bench in *Re Federenko*[4] in 1910. This arose from the killing by the accused of a watchman in a Russian village which was under martial law. The accused was a member of the Social Democrats, but it appeared that this was unknown to the arresting party which had been investigating the presence of strangers and called upon them to account for themselves. The Chief Justice inquired "Was the crime of the accused committed in the furtherance of a political object? He belonged to the social democratic party, whose object was, not only to alter the form of government, but also to do away with private ownership of property. A propaganda was carried on by them throughout the country and numerous revolutionary outrages were perpetrated by them. . . . [In view of the circumstances of the death,] can it be said that this killing was in furtherance of a political object? I think not. Nor do I think the fact that the crime of the accused would, in the demanding State, be called a political crime and be tried by a special tribunal makes it a crime of a political character within the meaning of the [Anglo-Russian Treaty, 1886]. The crime of killing a policeman by a person in no way identified with any political movement would in Russia be so described, and would be tried by same tribunal."

In Anglo-American practice it has come to be accepted that political offences are frequently committed as part and parcel of a violent attempt to overthrow the existing government and take over the reins of the state for the movement with which the potential asylee is associated. It is of the essence of such an act, however, that it cannot be committed by way of private

[3] *Recueil Officiel*, xvii, consid. 2, p. 455 (c. Papadatos, *Le Délit Politique*, 1954, p. 84).
[4] (1910) 17 C.C.C. 268; 15 W.L.R. 369.

enterprise, but must be part of an organised attempt. In summing up the practice of the United States, Hyde pointed out that "in every case . . . there has been an uprising . . . against the demanding government. . . . The accused has been connected with the movement . . . [and] either the acts charged against the accused have been deemed incidental to the movement, or the evidence has failed to show that the acts committed in the course of the uprising which might possibly not be justly regarded as incidental thereto, were in fact committed by the accused."[5] This view of the need for a "movement" was maintained by American courts even after those in England had apparently temporarily abandoned the rule in *Castioni*. At the same time, however, the United States authorities have found it possible to extend asylum to fugitives who might appear to be not entitled by the above definition, by ruling that there was no longer a treaty of extradition, even though it had only shortly before been held that a similar treaty still existed.[6]

Civil law countries, too, have adopted a somewhat similar attitude. Thus, in *Re Campara*,[7] 1957, the Chilean Supreme Court held that "according to generally accepted principles a political offence is one involving any attempt against the political organisation of the State or the political rights of its citizens, that is, an attack upon the constitutional order of the country concerned. This definition also comprehends acts which have as their objective a change in the established political or social order of the country." But perhaps the most comprehensive judicial statement on the matter is to be found in the decision of the Grenoble Appellate Tribunal in *Re Giovanni Gatti*,[8] 1947: "Political offences are those which injure the political organism, which are directed against the constitution of the Government and against sovereignty, which trouble the order established by the fundamental laws of the

[5] Hyde, *International Law*, vol. 2, 1947, pp. 1021-2.
[6] Compare Czech hijacking incident, 1950 (6 Whiteman, *Digest of International Law*, 1968, pp. 808-11) with *Karadzole* v. *Artukovic* (1957) 247 F. 2d. 198.
[7] 24 *Int. Law Reports*, p. 518, at 520.
[8] 14 *Annual Digest* (1947), pp. 145-6.

state and disturb the distribution of powers. Acts which aim at overthrowing or modifying the organisation of the main organs of the state, or at destroying, weakening or bring into disrepute one of these authorities, or at exercising illegitimate pressure on the play of their mechanism or on their general direction of the state, or which aim at changing the social conditions created for individuals by the constitution in one or all its elements, are also political offences. In brief, what distinguishes the political crime from the common crime is the fact that the former only affects the political organisation of the state, the proper rights of the state, while the latter exclusively affects rights other than those of the state. The fact that the reasons of sentiment which prompted the offender to commit the offence belong to the realm of politics does not itself create a political offence. The offence does not derive its political character from the motive of the offender but from the nature of the rights it injures. The reasons on which non-extradition is based do not permit the taking into account of mere motives for the purpose of attributing to a common crime the character of a political offence."

If this were all, there would be no doubt that aerial hijacking, whatever the motives activating it, could never be considered a political offence exempting the hijacker from extradition, provided a treaty to this effect exists between the two states involved. However, English judicial practice temporarily threw a new and apparently more liberal interpretation upon the concept, seemingly based on the fugitive's motive rather than on the character of the offence itself. *Re Kolczynski*[9] concerned a number of Polish seamen who had mutinied, brought their vessel to a British port and claimed that, although they were not part of an organised political movement seeking to overthrow their government, as political fugitives from their country they were entitled to asylum and exempt from the Anglo-Polish Extradition Treaty. The mutineers maintained that if they returned to Poland they would be subjected to political persecution, and the Lord Chief Justice said that "the revolt of the crew was to prevent themselves

[9] [1955] 1 Q.B. 540, 550, 551.

130

being prosecuted for a political offence and . . . therefore the offence had a political character." He pointed out that in the prevailing political conditions in Poland organized political movements were impossible so that the seamen could not fall within the terms of the *Castioni* definition, but he maintained that in that case the court was "not giving an exhaustive definition of the words of a political character . . . [and therefore he felt free to hold that] the evidence about the law prevalent in the Republic of Poland today shows that it is necessary if only for reasons of humanity, to give a wider and more generous meaning to the words we are now construing, which we can do without in any way encouraging the idea that ordinary crimes which have no political significance will be thereby excused." Only two years after this decision was rendered, the United States Circuit Court of Appeals acknowledged that this decision had been rendered, but based its own approach on the *Castioni* definition the language of which it pointed out had been adopted by American courts.[10] In a later hearing in the same case, the Commissioner used language which might have appeared in a nineteenth century judgment. Of the political offence, he said that "generally speaking it is an offense against the government itself or incident to political uprisings. It is not a political offense because the crime was committed by a politician. The crime must be incidental to and form part of political disturbances. *It must be in furtherance of one side or another of a bona fide struggle for political power.*"[11]

This somewhat rigid approach by the American courts is perhaps the more surprising in view of the fact that in 1957 Congress enacted legislation whereby visas left over from the Refugee Relief Act, 1953, could be issued on a nonquota basis to "refugee-escapes", that is to say "any alien who, because of persecution or fear of persecution on account of race, religion or political opposition has fled or shall flee from any Communist dominated, or Communist-occupied area. . ." This is in many ways the counterpart of provisions to be found in the

[10] *Karadzole* v. *Artukovic* (1957) 247 F.2d. 198, 203.
[11] *U.S., ex rel. Karadzole* v. *Artukovic* (1959) 170 F. Supp. 383, 392 (italics added).

constitutions of the various People's Republics. Thus, according to Article 129 of the Soviet Constitution, the Soviet Union "affords the right of asylum to foreign citizens persecuted for defending the interests of the working people, or for scientific activities, or for struggling for national liberation".

However, the American legislation is not as wide as one might be led to expect from its language, or from the reaction caused at the end of 1970 when a coastguard vessel denied asylum to a seaman from a Russian vessel and returned him whence he had come. A number of Yugoslav seamen sought to take advantage of the Act having deserted their ships when in American ports. In *Dunat* v. *Hurney*[12] the petitioner contended that he would be physically persecuted if he returned to Yugoslavia since he would be denied the opportunity to earn his living because of his Catholic beliefs. The Department of Immigration took the view that physical persecution involved death, torture or confinement on account of race, religion or political persuasion, but the Circuit Court of Appeals held that "the denial of an opportunity to earn a livelihood . . . is the equivalent of a sentence of death by means of slow starvation and none the less final because it is gradual." On reargument, a court of eight judges affirmed this, pointing out that "economic prescription so severe as to deprive a person of all means of earning a livelihood may amount to physical persecution." While this approach has apparently been accepted by the government, the issue is purely one of fact and depends on the evidence produced to show that economic deprivation would in fact follow,[13] and evidence that the petitioner might suffer "difficulties" with regard to such things as church attendance would not suffice, nor would he be protected simply on the ground that if he returned he would be tried for desertion.[14] Nor for that matter would the Act extend to cover one who had left a Communist country simply because he disliked or disapproved of the Communist Party or the government.[15] These cases refer to individuals

[12] (1961) 297 F.2d. 744, 746, 753.
[13] *Soric* v. *Flagg* (1962) 303 F.2d. 289.
[14] *Diminich* v. *Esperdy* (1961) 299 F.2d. 244, 247.
[15] *Morin* v. *Bouchard* (1962) 311 F. 2d. 181.

132

seeking asylum against whom no allegation that they have been involved in criminal offences — other than the act of flight — have been levelled. If they are not entitled to asylum, how much less are those who hijack an aircraft in order to leave a country the government of which they disapprove.

The German Federal Republic has been faced with somewhat similar problems as has the United States. By Article 16 of the Basic Law of the German Federal Republic "persons persecuted for political reasons shall enjoy the right of asylum". According to the Federal Constitutional Court,[16] "the legislative history shows that the right of political asylum was understood as 'a right granted to a foreigner who cannot continue living in his own country because he is deprived of liberty, life or property by the political system prevailing there'. *The concept of political persecution must not be narrowly interpreted.* It is characterised by deep-seated sociopolitical and ideological contrasts between states which have developed basically different internal structures. There are a number of states in which, for the purpose of enforcing and securing political and social revolutions, the power of the state is exercised in a manner contradictory to the principles of a liberal democracy. Hence *the concept of political persecutee must not be limited to so-called political offenders* within the meaning of the Extradition Law, i.e., to persons whose extradition is demanded by reason of a criminal act as defined in that law, *but must be extended to person prosecuted for non-political offenses 'where such persons, if extradired, would be liable in their home country to suffer measures of persecution involving danger to life and limb or restrictions of personal liberty for political reasons'.* A person can be a political persecutee even if he did not creat the facts justifying fear of persecution prior to his coming to the Federal Republic. Such cases must, however, be scrutinised very carefully, for foreigners must not be encouraged to create subsequently the conditions for the right of asylum for the sole purposes of obtaining protection from punishment for an ordinary crime."

The *caveat* embodied in this judgment has proved of im-

[16] Decision of Feb. 4, 1959, summarised in 54 A.J.I.L. 1960, p. 416, at pp. 417-8 (italics added).

portance in practice and has enabled the Federal Republic to pursue a somewhat similar policy to the United States in regard to requests by "refugees" for hospitality. Thus, the German authorities have refused to grant asylum to a Hungarian student whose study visa had terminated, but who contended that he and his father were opposed to the Hungarian Communist régime, or to those who have come to be described as "economic refugees" and are regarded as being in search of better jobs rather than as political fugitives from Communist governments.[17]

The more liberal approach of the English court was somewhat shortlived and in 1962 there was a return to the well-established and generally accepted *Castioni* principle. *Schtraks* v. *Government of Israel*[18] concerned an Israeli request for the return of an alleged child-kidnapper who contended that the abduction was at the instruction of the child's grandfather and related to the religious education of the child, arguing that religious issues and schooling were political questions in Israel and that as a political offender he should not be extradited. Lord Reid referred to the political and philosophical views prevailing at the time of the enactment of the English Extradition Act, and felt that in the instant case "there is nothing to indicate that [the appellant] acted as he did in order to force or even promote a change government policy, or to achieve a political objective of any kind". Both Viscount Radcliffe and Lord Hodson referred to the decisions in *Castioni, Meunier* and *Kolczynski*, with the former pointing out that the two nineteenth century cases required political motivation and contesting parties, and that the matter had rested thus until the Polish Seamen's Case: "But the decision seems to me to show only that the courts are unwilling to treat what was said in *Re Castioni* as laying down any exhaustive definition of 'political offence'. Certainly it would have been difficult to decide in favour of the fugitive in that case if it were always necessary to find a 'disturbance' in being reflecting an uprising, insurrection or other struggle for State

[17] *The Times* (London), Nov. 9, 1965.
[18] [1964] A.C. 556, 584, 591-2, 612 ([1962] 3 W.L.R. 1013).

134

power. On the other hand, if . . . the idea of 'political offence' is not altogether remote from that of 'political asylum', it is easy to regard as a political offence, an offence committed by someone in furtherance of his design to escape from a political régime which he found intolerable. I have no criticism to make of the decision in . . . *Kolczynski*, but the grounds on which it was decided are expressed too generally to offer much guidance for other cases in the future. . . . The idea that lies behind the phrase 'offence of a political character' is that the fugitive is at odds with the State that applies for his extradition on some issue connected with the political control or government of the country. The analogy of 'political' in this connection is with 'political' in such phrases as 'political refugee', 'political asylum' or 'political prisoner'. It does indicate . . . that the demanding State is after him for reasons other than the enforcement of the criminal law in its ordinary, . . . its common or international, aspect. It is this idea that the judges were seeking to express in . . . *Castioni* and *Meunier* when they connected the political offence with an uprising, a disturbance, an insurrection, a civil war or struggle for power: and . . . it is still necessary to maintain the idea of that connection. It is not departed from by taking a liberal view as to what is meant by disturbance or those other words, provided that the idea of political opposition as between fugitive and requesting State is not lost sight of: but it would be lost sight of . . . if one were to say that all offences were political offences, so long as they could be shown to have been committed for a political object with a political motive or for the furtherance of some political cause or campaign. There may, for instance, be all sorts of contending political organisations or forces in a country and members of them may commit all sorts of infractions of the criminal law in the belief that by so doing they will further their political ends: but if the central government stands apart and is concerned only to enforce the criminal law that has been violated by these contestants, I see no reason why fugitives should be protected by this country from its jurisdiction on the ground that they are political offenders. . . . This case has evidently become to some extent a political issue. But the evidence does not suggest that the appellant's offences . . . were committed against, as a demonstration against any policy of the Government of Israel itself or that he has been abetting those who oppose the Government . . ." Lord Hodson dealt with the issue fairly peremptorily: ". . . According to [the *Castioni*] test there must be either in existence or in contemplation a struggle between the State and the fugitive criminal. I prefer to adhere as far as possible to the guidance which I find in the *Castioni* case, judgment in which was delivered . . . not long after the passing of the first Extradition Act. It may be that cases will arise as in the *Polish Seamens's* case, where special considerations have to be taken into account. In some modern States politics and justice may be inextricably mixed, and it is not always easy, for example, to say what amounts to a revolt against the Government. No special feature exists in this case, and I find no substance in the contention that extradition should be refused because of the political character of the offence charged. . . "

From what has been said it would seem that *prima facie* aerial hijacking, at least when committed by an individual seeking to leave his country, cannot qualify as a political offence for which he is entitled to claim asylum. But is this a general rule?

Not all fugitives seeking political asylum have committed crimes as part of their political activity, although the states from which they have fled frequently assert that whatever else may be the reason for their flight it is also because there have been criminal charges laid against them. Often the state of refuge has considered the latter allegation to be untrue and has claimed the right to afford asylum to those whom it wishes, provided there is no ground for an extradition process being instituted. Perhaps the only occasion on which an aerial hijacker might be able to claim that no offence of any kind was committed in the course of his flight, other than unlawful departure, would be when he was piloting an aircraft belonging to the state or a flying club or to some other private individual who had permitted him to fly, contending that he had not intention of keeping the aircraft and used it merely as the means of escape. The more normal type of hijacking with which we have become acquainted in recent years has involved the seizure or deviation of an aircraft being used for passenger or military purposes, necessitating interference with the freedom of movement of the persons on board or the endangering of the machine which has frequently been state property.

Over the past few years a practice has grown up among most countries, both those subscribing to the principles of western democracy and those committed to the principles of marxist-leninism, whereby their governments reserve to themselves the right to afford asylum to those aliens who claim that they have fled their homeland for political reasons, and against whom no charges of being involved in common crimes have been alleged. But such discretion does not appear to have been completely unlimited. It tends to be exercised on the basis that the fugitive is in fact in danger of his life or his freedom because of his opposition to the established régime of the country from which he has fled. Frequently, too, it has been exercised in favour of those who allege that the persecution they fear is stemming from a country which is potentially or actually politically unfriendly from the point of view of the country of refuge. This would suggest that, applying the type of principle mentioned earlier in connection with the immigration regulations of the United States and the Federal German Republic, those who have hijacked an aircraft to enable them to leave a country with whose political system they are not in sympathy would almost certainly not be regarded as political offenders by the majority of the countries in the world. On the other hand, one must remember that the People's Democracies declare their willingness to afford asylum to anyone fleeing because he is persecuted on account of his democratic principles, and this affords an easy excuse to give hospitality to a number of those who have hijacked aircraft to leave the United States. In so far as deserters from the armed forces or military draft-dogers are concerned, the position may be different, for most countries are unwilling to extradite or otherwise return those who are accused of military offences.

The real problem, however, relates to the hijacking of aircraft which involves danger to passengers, crew, machines, or other aircraft due to interference with normal flight rules. On March 24, 1950, three Czech aircraft carrying 85 persons were liverted in flight and landed at an airfield in the United States Zone of Occupation in Germany. Apparently in two of the cases members of the crew were threatened, manhandled and tied, while in the third case the deviation was carried out by the crew. The Czech authorities contended that the hijackers should be returned, maintaining that they had committed crimes contrary to the Czech Penal Code, namely, endangering the lives of passengers and crew, unjustifiably limiting personal freedom and kidnapping. The United States replied that the treaties in force between itself and Czechoslovakia could not apply to effect return of anybody in the United States Zone of Occupation, and, since extradition only existed by right of treaty, there were no grounds for returning the alleged criminals. Furthermore, "it is clear that these individuals fled Czechoslovakia for political reasons by whatever means they could find to escape. It has never been the practice of the United States Government to take action which would have the effect of subjecting political offenders to criminal jurisdiction. . . . The United States Government [pursuing a principle which has been followed since 1853], therefore, sees no reason to assist in the enforcement of Czechoslovak internal law by returning the accused in this case. As a matter of comity, the United States authorities endeavoured, of course, to return to Czechoslovakia, as promptly as all necessary arrangements could be completed, persons from the planes who expressed a desire to return. The United States Government will continue strictly to observe such standards of international conduct. Comity, on the other hand, could not reasonably be construed to require the United States authorities to arrange for the return of those who were resolved to remain. In accordance with humanitarian principles, the latter have been given the right of policial asylum."[19] Only six months later the United States took the same stance with regard to Czechs who "hijacked" a train and crossed the border into the United States Occupation Zone.[20] Whatever may be one's view of the legality or morality of the United States position in these cases, it makes it difficult for the United States to put forward

[19] 6 Whiteman, *Digest of International Law,* 1968, pp. 810-1.
[20] *Ibid.,* pp. 811-2.

138

claims for the return of a hijacker who may have fled, say to Cuba, Chile or Algeria, and claims that he is a political fugitive from the United States and succeeds in persuading the local government, as part of its "anti-Americanism", to support his contention.

Some twenty years ago, as these Czech cases indicate, aerial hijacking seemed to be reserved to those who were fleeing their country and were seizing aircraft belonging to that country, and whose passengers possessed the same nationality as themselves. This sort of factual situation lends credence to any contention that the act was political and is in accord with the decision of the Swiss Federal Tribunal of April 30, 1952.[21] A Yugoslav passenger aircraft had been diverted to Switzerland by three crew members. The Yugoslav Government sought their extradition on the basis of the Swiss-Serbian Treaty of 1897, claiming that the fugitives had subjected the other crew members to unlawful constraint, as well as having endangered the safety of public transport and wrongfully appropriated property. In the court's view, "all the offences with which the accused are charged were means to effectuate their escape abroad, and coincided completely with that escape. The question must therefore be examined whether that escape constituted a purely political offence; if so, extradition must be refused on the ground that the offences for which it is requested are not only connected with a purely political offence, but also constitute such an offence. . . . The purpose and motive of the acts with which the accused are charged was to enable them to flee from a country with whose régime they were not in agreement and where they felt themselves to be watched and repressed. . . . This fact gives both the flight and the offences committed to make it possible a distinctly political colouring. That is not, however, enough to exclude the possibility of extradition for these offences; it is also necessary that their political character should outweigh their common characteristics. . . . The Federal Tribunal [has given] a restrictive interpretation to the concept of relative political offences, and required, in particular, that the act should be re-

[21] *In re Kavic, Bjelanovic and Arsenijevic*, 19 *Int. Law Reports*, p. 371, at 373-4 (italics added).

lated to a general activity directly aimed at the realization of political aims, and should have been committed in the framework of a fight for political power. This applies to the flight of a political opponent from the country only if it is intended to continue the fight for power from abroad. . . . *That restrictive interpretation does not,* however, bear re-examination; it does not meet the intention of the [Extradition] Law [of 1892], nor *take account of recent historical developments, such as the growth of totalitarian States.* In such States all political opposition is suppressed and a fight for power is, if not impossible from the start, at least practically without any chance of success. Those who do not wish to submit to the régime have no alternative but to escape it by flight abroad. . . . This more passive attitude for the purpose of escaping political constraint is no less worthy of asylum than active participation in the fight for political power used to be in what were earlier considered to be normal circumstances. The spirit of justice undoubtedly ascribes a political character to such a flight abroad, and a liberalization of the practice of this Court, with a view to adjusting it to recent developments, appears justified. In matters of extradition in particular, the Court must not abandon that spirit in favour of legalistic considerations, and must take account of historical and political developments. . . . Recent practice has been too restrictive in making the relative political character of an offence dependent on its commission in the framework of a fight for power. Such a character must also be attributed to offences which were committed in order to escape the constraint of a State which makes all opposition and, therefore, the fight for power impossible. In this connection *there can also be applied the principle that the relation between the purpose and the means adopted* for its achievement *must be* such that the ideals connected with the purpose are *sufficiently strong to excuse, if not justify, the injury* to private property, *and to make the offender appear worthy of asylum.* Freedom from the constraint of a totalitarian State must be regarded as an ideal in this sense. In the present case the required relationship undoubtedly exists; for, on the one hand, the offences against the other members of the crew were not very serious, and, on

140

the other, political freedom and even existence of the accused was at stake, and could only be achieved through the commission of these offences."

Not only did the Swiss court adopt a subjective view as to the desirability of one way of political life over another, but it implied the decision could well have been different if the injuries involved had been more serious or if the desire to escape had not justified the extreme risks involved, so that there was no longer a proper relation between the purpose desired and the means employed. Many of the more recent—and more spectacular—hijackings would not appear to fall within the Swiss confines. On the one hand, large numbers of civilian passengers have been placed at risk, while on the other the aircraft involved has frequently not belonged to the country from which flight has taken place or against which demonstration is being made.

To date, all cases in which political asylum has been granted or in which a court has been prepared to hold that an offence is of a political character, qualifying the accused for asylum and exemption from extradition, have been directed solely against the country from which the offender has fled—and this has been true whether the definition of "political" has been based on the *Castioni* ruling or the more liberal attitude expressed in *Kolczynski*, by the Swiss Federal Court or by the United States Government towards Czechoslovakia. It is difficult to see how a case may be made to allege that the hijacking of an aircraft belonging to one country can amount to a political offence directed against a third country, whether this be the country of which the hijackers is a national, or with which his country or the political organisation with which he is associated regards itself as at war or engaged in hostilities not amounting to war in the sense of international law. This would clearly exclude from any claim to political asylum such persons as the Arab guerrillas who recently hijacked—and in some cases destroyed—"neutral" aircraft in order to bring their cause to the notice of the world in a dramatic fashion, or to bring pressure upon the neutral country so that it in its turn might pressurise Israel, or to bring pressure upon Israel because some of the passengers on board the aircraft in question were

Israeli citizens or Jews of another nationality, but for whom Israel might feel some moral responsibility. Such forms of hijacking are no more "political" in the sense that has been accepted to date than the kidnapping of a neutral diplomat in order to exact concessions from the State to which the latter has been accredited. While the kidnapping of a local politician might amount to a political action warranting a grant of asylum, this might also be true if the hijacked aircraft was a State aircraft belonging to the country against which the hijackers were directing their political activities, or belonged to a State which was in sympathy with such a State, and perhaps even if it were a civil aircraft belonging to the politically opposed state if all the passengers on board were co-nationals.

This latter proposition, however, calls to mind the hint to be found in the Swiss judgment concerning the relation between end and means and the gravity of the injury caused in order to effect the escape. It could be argued that to hijack a passenger aircraft with a number of civilians on board, and particularly when some of those passengers might have a tendency to become "trigger-happy" in an attempt to foil the hijacking, far outweighs even an attempt to escape even when not to escape might endanger the life of the person involved. After all, many systems of municipal law, as well as international law, do not recognise personal safety as justifying what would otherwise constitute a criminal act, as is to be seen with the attitude adopted towards the defence of superior orders to an alleged war crime. The passengers on board a hijacked aircraft are clearly at risk, especially as the crew are often held at gunpoint and are never free agents, while the diversion may involve an extra flight distance that renders the aircraft mechanically a danger, as well as perhaps interfering with other flight routes. If this is so with a person trying to flee to save his life or to secure what he considers to be a better way of life, it should apply even more so to a hijacker who is not seeking thus to secure his political freedom, but is endeavouring to effect some political action against the country under whose law the aircraft has been registered, or some third country. In fact, when civilian passengers are involved, a strong case could be made to apply the same re-

142

strictive principle even though the hijacked aircraft possesses the nationality of the country against which the demonstration is intended.

It is true that it may happen that in cases of the kind here mentioned, no extradition treaties may exist between the country to which the hijacked aircraft has been taken and the country of aircraft registration, or with the country of the nationality of individual passengers, and it may be that there is some doubt as to which country, if any, actually had jurisdiction over the aircraft at the precise moment of seizure. Since there is no rule of customary international law providing for the extradition of criminals, none of the countries involved would be under any direct legal obligations or possessed of any legal rights. However, just as there is no duty to extradite in the absence of treaty, so there is no duty to afford political asylum to anybody. Popular parlance has already tended to regard aircraft hijacking as a form of piracy — in fact the International Law Association has done the same — and it may well be that in this case too there should be some measure of universal jurisdiction, with the country from which asylum is sought, or in which the hijackers find themselves, being under a clear obligation to subject the hijacker to its own criminal processes, as Denmark has already done, unless it is prepared to return such person to a country willing to invoke its criminal jurisdiction, and if more than one country is involved it should not be excessively difficult to apply the principle of the "closest link".

The problem of aerial hijacking, like that of diplomatic kidnapping, has become of such significance that it probably cannot be adequately dealt with on a bilateral basis, any more than could the submarine "piracy" that was dealt with by the Nyon Agreement. Efforts to ensure international action have not been lacking, even though as yet they may not have been very effective. On November 18, 1970, the Sixth (Legal) Committee of the Twenty-fifth General Assembly of the United Nations adopted two resolutions concerning Aerial Hijacking or Interference with Civil Air Traffic. By a vote of 99 in favour, with none against and 10 abstentions, it was agreed to condemn aerial hijacking, to call upon states to "provide for the prosecution and punishment of persons who perpetrate such acts, in a manner commensurate with the gravity of those crimes, or, without prejudice to the rights and obligations of States under existing international instruments relating to the matter, for the extradition of such persons" so that they might stand trial, condemned the taking of hostages or the unlawful detention of passengers or crew, and called for concerted action. It is true that this Resolution, while calling for prosecution, said nothing about political asylum, but the Committee agreed that this resolution "cannot prejudice any international legal rights or duties of States under instruments relating to the status of refugees and other stateless persons". It would be interesting to know why it was felt that refugees or stateless persons who hijack aircraft should be treated in any way differently from hijackers possessing a nationality. The Legal Committee's resolution also called upon States to make every effort to ensure that the diplomatic conference on this subject being held at The Hague a month later should prove successful. The Convention for the Suppression of Unlawful Seizure of Aircraft was adopted on December 16, 1970, and requires each contracting state to treat hijacking as a punishable offence and to take measures to establish its jurisdiction when the offence is committed on an aircraft carrying its registration, when the aircraft lands on its territory with the hijacker on board, or when the aircraft without crew has been leased to a lessee having his principal place of business or permanent residence in that state. The Convention also stipulates that states shall provide for the exercise of their jurisdiction when the alleged offender is found in their territory. Should the state concerned not be willing to try the offender, then it shall be obliged to extradite and the convention requires hijacking to be included in all future extradition treaties, or if no treaty exists then the convention will itself serve as the legal basis for creating this obligation. When extradition is not granted, there is an obligation to prosecute locally. Although the Convention provides that the state in which the offender is found shall, if it does not extradite him, "be obliged, without exception whatsoever, [presumably rejecting any ground for asylum] and whether or not the offence was

144

committed in its territory" to prosecute itself, it does provide that it shall "not apply to aircraft used in military, customs or police services", which is in accordance with normal practice.

The Convention requires ratification and also, in most cases, amendments to municipal law. In fact, the Government of Canada immediately announced that it was examining the terms of the Convention with a view to ascertaining what legislation would be required in order to make it effective under Canadian law. Unfortunately, practice shows that it is frequently difficult to secure the ratification of a multilateral treaty and even more difficult when legislative changes are necessary. Nevertheless, it is submitted that, even if the Convention does not become effective, there is in international law as it now exists no basis for extending asylum to aerial hijackers.

Appendix 1

TOKYO CONVENTION 1963

The Convention on Offences and certain other Acts Committed on board Aircraft

Tokyo, 14 September, 1963
The States Parties to this Convention
Have agreed as follows:

Chapter I. *Scope of the Convention*

Article 1
(1) This Convention shall apply in respect of:
(a) offences against penal law;
(b) acts which, whether or not they are offences, may or do jeopardise the safety of the aircraft or of persons or property therein or which jeopardise good order and discipline on board.

(2) Except as provided in Chapter III, this Convention shall apply in respect of offences committed or acts done by a person on board any aircraft registered in a Contracting State, while that aircraft is in flight or on the surface of the high seas or of any other area outside the territory of any State.

(3) For the purposes of this Convention, an aircraft is considered to be in flight from the moment when power is applied for the purpose of take-off until the moment when the landing run ends.

(4) This Convention shall not apply to aircraft used in military, customs or police services.

Article 2

Without prejudice to the provisions of Article 4 and except when the safety of the aircraft or of persons or property on board so requires, no provision of this Convention shall be interpreted as authorising or requiring any action in respect of offences against penal laws of a political nature or those based on racial or religious discrimination.

Chapter II. *Jurisdiction*

Article 3

(1) The State of registration of the aircraft is competent to exercise jurisdiction over offences and acts committed 'on board.

(2) Each Contracting State shall take such measures as may be necessary to establish its jurisdiction as the State of registration over offences committed on board aircraft registered in such State.

(3) This Convention does not exclude any criminal jurisdiction exercised in accordance with national law.

Article 4

A Contracting State which is not the State of registration may not interfere with an aircraft in flight in order to exercise its criminal jurisdiction over an offence committed on board except in the following cases:

(a) the offence has effect on the territory of such State;

(b) the offence has been committed by or against a national or permanent resident of such State;

(c) the offence is against the security of such State;

(d) the offence consists of a breach of any rules or regulations relating to the flight or manoeuvre of aircraft in force in such State;

(e) the exercise of jurisdiction is necessary to ensure the observance of any obligation of such State under a multilateral international agreement.

Chapter III. *Powers of the Aircraft Commander*

Article 5

(1) The provisions of this Chapter shall not apply to offences and acts committed or about to be committed by a person on board an aircraft in flight in the airspace of the State of registration or over the high seas or any other area outside the territory of any State unless the last point of take-off or the next point of intended landing is situated in a State other than that of registration, or the aircraft subsequently flies in the airspace of a State other than that of registration with such person still on board.

(2) Notwithstanding the provisions of Article 1, paragraph (3), an aircraft shall for the purposes of this Chapter, be considered to be in flight at any time from the moment when all its external doors are closed following embarkation until the moment when any such door is opened for disembarkation. In the case of a forced landing, the provisions of this Chapter shall continue to apply with respect to offences and acts committed on board until competent authorities of a State take over the responsibility for the aircraft and for the persons and property on board.

Article 6

(1) The aircraft commander may, when he has reasonable grounds to believe that a person has committed, or is about to commit, on board the aircraft, an offence or act contemplated in Article 1, paragraph (1), impose upon such person reasonable measures including restraint which are necessary:

(a) to protect the safety of the aircraft, or of persons or property therein; or

(b) to maintain good order and discipline on board; or

(c) to enable him to deliver such person to competent authorities or to disembark him in accordance with the provisions of this Chapter.

(2) The aircraft commander may require or authorise the assistance of other crew members and may request or authorise, but not require, the assistance of passengers to restrain any person whom he is entitled to restrain. Any crew member

149

or passenger may also take reasonable preventive measures without such authorisation when he has reasonable grounds to believe that such action is immediately necessary to protect the safety of the aircraft, or of persons or property therein.

Article 7

(1) Measures of restraint imposed upon a person in accordance with Article 6 shall not be continued beyond any point at which the aircraft lands unless:

(a) such point is in the territory of a non-Contracting State and its authorities refuse to permit disembarkation of that person or those measures have been imposed in accordance with Article 6, paragraph (1) (c) in order to enable his delivery to competent authorities;

(b) the aircraft makes a forced landing and the aircraft commander is unable to deliver that person to competent authorities; or

(c) that person agrees to onward carriage under restraint.

(2) The aircraft commander shall as soon as practicable, and if possible before landing in the territory of a State with a person on board who has been placed under restraint in accordance with the provisions of Article 6, notify the authorities of such State of the fact that a person on board is under restraint and of the reasons for such restraint.

Article 8

(1) The aircraft commander may, in so far as it is necessary for the purpose of subparagraph (a) or (b) of paragraph (1) of Article 6, disembark in the territory of any State in which the aircraft lands any person who he has reasonable grounds to believe has committed, or is about to commit, on board the aircraft an act contemplated in Article 1, paragraph (1) (b).

(2) The aircraft commander shall report to the authorities of the State in which he disembarks any person pursuant to this Article, the fact of, and the reasons for, such disembarkation.

Article 9

(1) The aircraft commander may deliver to the competent authorities of any Contracting State in the territory of which the aircraft lands any person who he has reasonable grounds to believe has committed on board the aircraft an act which, in his opinion, is a serious offence according to the penal law of the State of registration of the aircraft.

(2) The aircraft commander shall as soon as practicable and if possible before landing in the territory of a Contracting State with a person on board whom the aircraft commander intends to deliver in accordance with the preceding paragraph, notify the authorities of such State of his intention to deliver such person and the reasons therefor.

(3) The aircraft commander shall furnish the authorities to whom any suspected offender is delivered in accordance with the provisions of this Article with evidence and information which, under the law of the State of registration of the aircraft, are lawfully in his possession.

Article 10

For actions taken in accordance with this Convention, neither the aircraft commander, any other member of the crew, any passenger, the owner or operator of the aircraft, nor the person on whose behalf the flight was performed shall be held responsible in any proceeding on account of the treatment undergone by the person against whom the actions were taken.

Chapter IV. *Unlawful Seizure of Aircraft*

Article 11

(1) When a person on board has unlawfully committed by force or threat thereof an act of interference, seizure, or other wrongful exercise of control of an aircraft in flight or when such an act is about to be committed, Contracting States shall take all appropriate measures to restore control of the aircraft to its lawful commander or to preserve his control of the aircraft.

(2) In the cases contemplated in the preceding paragraph, the Contracting State in which the aircraft lands shall permit its passengers and crew to continue their journey as soon as practicable, and shall return the aircraft and its cargo to the persons lawfully entitled to possession.

Chapter V. *Powers and Duties of States*

Article 12

Any Contracting State shall allow the commander of an aircraft registered in another Contracting State to disembark any person pursuant to Article 8, paragraph (1).

Article 13

(1) Any Contracting State shall take delivery of any person whom the aircraft commander delivers pursuant to Article 9, paragraph (1).

(2) Upon being satisfied that the circumstances so warrant, any Contracting State shall take custody or other measures to ensure the presence of any person suspected of an act contemplated in Article 11, paragraph (1), and of any person of whom it has taken delivery. The custody and other measures shall be as provided in the law of that State but may only be continued for such time as is reasonably necessary to enable any criminal or extradition proceedings to be instituted.

(3) Any person in custody pursuant to the previous paragraph shall be assisted in communicating immediately with the nearest appropriate representative of the State of which he is a national.

(4) Any Contracting State, to which a person is delivered pursuant to Article 9, paragraph (1), or in whose territory an aircraft lands following the commission of an act contemplated in Article 11, paragraph (1), shall immediately make a preliminary enquiry into the facts.

(5) When a State, pursuant to this Article, has taken a person into custody, it shall immediately notify the State of registration of the aircraft and the State of nationality of the detained person and, if it considers it advisable, any other

interested State of the fact that such person is in custody and of the circumstances which warrant his detention. The State which makes the preliminary enquiry contemplated in paragraph (4) of this Article shall promptly report its findings to the said States and shall indicate whether it intends to exercise jurisdiction.

Article 14

(1) When any person has been disembarked in accordance with Article 8, paragraph (1), or delivered in accordance with Article 9, paragraph (1), or has disembarked after committing an act contemplated in Article 11, paragraph (1), and when such person cannot or does not desire to continue his journey and the State of landing refuses to admit him, that State may, if the person in question is not a national or permanent resident of that State, return him to the territory of the State of which he is a national or permanent resident or to the territory of the State in which he began his journey by air.

(2) Neither disembarkation, nor delivery, nor the taking of custody or other measures contemplated in Article 13, paragraph (2), nor return of the person concerned, shall be considered as admission to the territory of the Contracting State concerned for the purpose of its law relating to entry or admission of persons and nothing in this Convention shall affect the law of a Contracting State relating to the expulsion of persons from its territory.

Article 15

(1) Without prejudice to Article 14, any person who has been disembarked in accordance with Article 8, paragraph (1), or delivered in accordance with Article 9, paragraph (1), or has disembarked after committing an act contemplated in Article 11, paragraph (1), and who desires to continue his journey shall be at liberty as soon as practicable to proceed to any destination of his choice unless his presence is required by the law of the State of landing for the purpose of extradition or criminal proceedings.

(2) Without prejudice to its law as to entry and admission to, and extradition and expulsion from its territory, a Con-

tracting State in whose territory a person has been disembarked in accordance with Article 8, paragraph (1), or delivered in accordance with Article 9, paragraph (1), or has disembarked and is suspected of having committed an act contemplated in Article 11, paragraph (1), shall accord to such person treatment which is no less favourable for his protection and security than that accorded to nationals of such Contracting State in like circumstances.

Chapter VI. *Other Provisions*

Article 16

(1) Offences committed on aircraft registered in a Contracting State shall be treated, for the purpose of extradition, as if they had been committed not only in the place in which they have occurred but also in the territory of the State of registration of the aircraft.

(2) Without prejudice to the provisions of the preceding paragraph, nothing in this Convention shall be deemed to create an obligation to grant extradition.

Article 17

In taking any measures for investigation or arrest or otherwise exercising jurisdiction in connection with any offence committed on board an aircraft the Contracting States shall pay due regard to the safety and other interests of air navigation and shall so act as to avoid unnecessary delay of the aircraft, passengers, crew or cargo.

Article 18

If Contracting States establish joint air transport operating organisations or international operating agencies, which operate aircraft not registered in any one State those States shall, according to the circumstances of the case, designate the State among them which, for the purposes of this Convention, shall be considered as the State of registration and shall give notice thereof to the International Civil Aviation Organisation which shall communicate the notice to all States Parties to this Convention.

Chapter VII. *Final Clauses*

Article 19

Until the date on which this Convention comes into force in accordance with the provisions of Article 21, it shall remain open for signature on behalf of any State which at that date is a Member of the United Nations or of any of the Specialised Agencies.

Article 20

(1) This Convention shall be subject to ratification by the signatory States in accordance with their constitutional procedures.

(2) The instruments of ratification shall be deposited with the International Civil Aviation Organisation.

Article 21

(1) As soon as twelve of the signatory States have deposited their instruments of ratification of this Convention, it shall come into force between them on the ninetieth day after the date of the deposit of the twelfth instrument of ratification. It shall come into force for each State ratifying thereafter on the ninetieth day after the deposit of its instrument of ratification.

(2) As soon as this Convention comes into force, it shall be registered with the Secretary-General of the United Nations by the International Civil Aviation Organisation.

Article 22

(1) This Convention shall, after it has come into force, be open for accession by any State Member of the United Nations or of any of the Specialised Agencies.

(2) The accession of a State shall be effected by the deposit of an instrument of accession with the International Civil Aviation Organisation and shall take effect on the ninetieth day after the date of such deposit.

Article 23

(1) Any Contracting State may denounce this Convention by notification addressed to the International Civil Aviation Organisation.

(2) Denunciation shall take effect six months after the date of receipt by the International Civil Aviation Organisation of the notification of denunciation.

Article 24

(1) Any dispute between two or more Contracting States concerning the interpretation or application of this Convention which cannot be settled through negotiation, shall, at the request of one of them, be submitted to arbitration. If within six months from the date of the request for arbitration the Parties are unable to agree on the organisation of the arbitration, any one of those Parties may refer the dispute to the International Court of Justice by request in conformity with the Statute of the Court.

(2) Each State may at the time of signature or ratification of this Convention or accession thereto, declare that it does not consider itself bound by the preceding paragraph. The other Contracting States shall not be bound by the preceding paragraph with respect to any Contracting State having made such a reservation.

(3) Any Contracting State having made a reservation in accordance with the preceding paragraph may at any time withdraw this reservation by notification to the International Civil Aviation Organisation.

Article 25

Except as provided in Article 24 no reservation may be made to this Convention.

Article 26

The International Civil Aviation Organisation shall give notice to all States Members of the United Nations or of any of the Specialised Agencies:
(a) of any signature of this Convention and the date thereof;
(b) of the deposit of any instrument of ratification or accession and the date thereof;
(c) of the date on which this Convention comes into force in accordance with Article 21, paragraph (1);
(d) of the receipt of any notification of denunciation and the date thereof; and

(e) of the receipt of any declaration or notification made under Article 24 and the date thereof.

In witness whereof the undersigned Plenipotentiaries, having been duly authorised, have signed this Convention.

Done at Tokyo on the fourteenth day of September One Thousand Nine Hundred and Sixty-three in three authentic texts drawn up in the English, French and Spanish languages.

This Convention shall be deposited with the International Civil Aviation Organisation with which, in accordance with Article 19, it shall remain open for signature and the said Organisation shall send certified copies thereof to all States Members of the United Nations or of any Specialised Agency.

Appendix 2

CONVENTION ON THE HIGH SEAS, (GENEVA, 1958)

Article 14
All States shall co-operate to the fullest possible extent in the repression of piracy on the high seas or in any other place outside the jurisdiction of any State.

Article 15
Piracy consists of any of the following acts:
(1) Any illegal acts of violence, detention or any act of depredation, committed for private ends by the crew or the passengers of a private ship or a private aircraft, and directed:
(a) On the high seas, against another ship or aircraft, or against persons or property on board such ship or aircraft;
(b) Against a ship, aircraft, persons or property in a place outside the jurisdiction of any State;
(2) Any act of voluntary participation in the operation of a ship or of an aircraft with knowledge of facts making it a pirate ship or aircraft;
(3) Any act of inciting or of intentionally facilitating an act described in sub-paragraph 1 or sub-paragraph 2 of this article.

Article 16
The acts of piracy, as defined in article 15, committed by a warship, government ship or government aircraft whose crew has mutinied and taken control of the ship or aircraft are assimilated to acts committed by a private ship.

Article 17
A ship or aircraft is considered a pirate ship or aircraft if it is intended by the persons in dominant control to be used for the purpose of committing one of the acts referred to in article

15. The same applies if the ship or aircraft has been used to commit any such act, so long as it remains under the control of the persons guilty of that act.

Article 18

A ship or aircraft may retain its nationality although it has become a pirate ship or aircraft. The retention or loss of nationality is determined by the law of the State from which such nationality was originally derived.

Article 19

On the high seas, or in any other place outside the jurisdiction of any State, every State may seize a pirate ship or aircraft, or a ship taken by piracy and under the control of pirates, and arrest the persons and seize the property on board. The courts of the State which carried out the seizure may decide upon the penalties to be imposed, and may also determine the action to be taken with regard to the ships, aircraft or property, subject to the rights of third parties acting in good faith.

Article 20

Where the seizure of a ship or aircraft on suspicion or piracy has been effected without adequate grounds, the State making the seizure shall be liable to the State the nationality of which is possessed by the ship or aircraft, for any loss or damage caused by the seizure.

Article 21

A seizure on account of piracy may only be carried out by warships or military aircraft, or other ships or aircraft on government service authorized to that effect.

Article 22

1. Except where acts of interference derive from powers conferred by treaty, a warship which encounters a foreign merchant ship on the high seas is not justified in boarding her unless there is reasonable ground for suspecting:
(a) That the ship is engaged in piracy; or

(b) That the ship is engaged in the slave trade; or

(c) That, though flying a foreign flag or refusing to show its flag, the ship is, in reality, of the same nationality as the warship.

2. In the cases provided for in sub-paragraphs (a), (b) and (c) above, the warship may proceed to verify the ship's right to fly its flag. To this end, it may send a boat under the command of an officer to the suspected ship. If suspicion remains after the documents have been checked, it may proceed to a further examination on board the ship, which must be carried out with all possible consideration.

3. If the suspicions prove to be unfounded, and provided that the ship boarded has not committed any act justifying them, it shall be compensated for any loss or damage that may have been sustained.

Appendix 3

UNITED NATIONS GENERAL ASSEMBLY

Resolution on forcible diversion of civil Aircraft in flight
(Resolution 2551 (XXIV), December 12, 1969)

RESOLUTION ADOPTED BY THE GENERAL ASSEMBLY
[on the report of the Sixth Committee (A/7845)]

2551 (XXIV). *Forcible diversion of civil aircraft in flight*

THE GENERAL ASSEMBLY,

DEEPLY CONCERNED over acts of unlawful interference with international civil aviation,

CONSIDERING it necessary to recommend effective measures against hijacking in all its forms, or any other unlawful seizure or exercise of control of aircraft,

MINDFUL that such acts may endanger the life and health of passengers and crew in disregard of commonly accepted humanitarian considerations,

AWARE that international civil aviation can only function properly in conditions guaranteeing the safety of its operations and the due exercise of the freedom of air travel,

1. CALLS UPON States to take every appropriate measure to ensure that their respective national legislations provide an adequate framework for effective legal measures against all kinds of acts of unlawful interference with seizure of, or other wrongful exercise of control by force or threat thereof over, civil aircraft in flight;

2. URGES States in particular to ensure that persons on board who perpetrate such acts are prosecuted;

3. URGES full support for the efforts of the International Civil Aviation Organization directed towards the speedy pre-

161

paration and implementation of a convention providing for appropriate measures, *inter alia*, with respect to making the unlawful seizure of civil aircraft a punishable offence and to the prosecution of persons who commit that offence;

4. INVITES States to ratify or accede to the Convention on Offences and Certain Other Acts Committed on Board Aircraft, signed at Tokyo on 14 September 1963, in conformity with the Convention.

1831st plenary meeting,
12 December 1969

Appendix 4

ICAO LEGAL COMMITTEE

Draft Convention prepared by the Subcommittee on Unlawful Seizure of Aircraft

THE STATES PARTIES TO THIS CONVENTION

CONSIDERING that unlawful acts of seizure or exercise of control of aircraft in flight jeopardize the safety of persons and property, seriously affect the operation of international air services, and undermine the confidence of the peoples of the world in the safety of civil aviation;

CONSIDERING that the occurrence of such acts is a matter of grave concern;

CONSIDERING that for the purpose of deterring such acts, there is an urgent need to make them punishable as an offence and to provide for appropriate measures with respect to prosecution and extradition of offenders;

CONSIDERING, in consequence, that it is necessary to adopt provisions additional to those of international agreements in force and in particular to those of the Convention signed at Tokyo on 14 September 1963 on Offences and Certain Other Acts Committed on Board Aircraft,

HAVE AGREED AS FOLLOWS:

Article 1

Any person who on board an aircraft in flight:

(a) unlawfully, by force or threat thereof seizes or exercises control of that aircraft, or attempts to perform any such act, or

(b) is an accomplice of a person who performs or attempts to perform any such act,

commits an offence (hereinafter referred to as "the offence").

163

Article 2

1. For the purposes of this Convention, an aircraft is considered to be in flight from the moment when power is applied for the purpose of take-off until the moment when the landing run ends.

2. This Convention shall not apply to aircraft used in military, customs or police services.

3. This Convention shall not apply where the aircraft on board which the offence was committed neither took off nor landed outside the territory of the State of registration of that aircraft.

Article 3

Each Contracting State undertakes to make the offence punishable in a manner commensurate with the gravity of such offence.

Article 4

1. Each Contracting State shall take such measures as may be necessary to establish its jurisdiction over the offence in the following cases:
(a) when the offence is committed on board an aircraft registered in that State;
(b) when the aircraft lands and the alleged offender leaves the aircraft in its territory.

2. This Convention does not exclude any criminal jurisdiction exercised in accordance with national law.

Article 5

The Contracting States which establish joint air transport operating organizations or international operating agencies, which operate aircraft not registered in any one State, shall, according to the circumstances of the case, designate the State among them which, for the purposes of this Convention, shall be considered as the State of registration and shall give notice thereof to the International Civil Aviation Organization which shall communicate the notice to all States Parties to this Convention.

Article 6

1. Upon being satisfied that the circumstances so warrant, the Contracting State in the territory of which the aircraft lands and the alleged offender leaves the aircraft, shall take him into custody or take other measures to ensure his presence. The custody and other measures shall be as provided in the law of that State but may only be continued for such time as is reasonably necessary to enable any criminal or extradition proceedings to be instituted.

2. Such State shall immediately make a preliminary enquiry into the facts.

3. Any person in custody pursuant to paragraph 1 shall be assisted in communicating immediately with the nearest appropriate representative of the State of which he is a national.

4. When a State, pursuant to this Article, has taken a person into custody, it shall immediately notify the State of registration of the aircraft and the State of nationality of the detained person and, if it considers it advisable, any other interested States of the fact that such person is in custody and of the circumstances which warrant his detention. The State which makes the preliminary enquiry contemplated in paragraph 2 of this Article shall promptly report its findings to the said States and shall indicate whether it intends to exercise jurisdiction.

Article 7

The Contracting State which has taken measures pursuant to Article 6, paragraph 1, shall, if it does not extradite the alleged offender, be obliged to submit the case to its competent authorities for their decision whether legal proceedings should be initiated against him. These authorities shall take their decision in the same manner as in the case of other offences.

Article 8

1. The offence shall be deemed to be an extraditable offence in any extradition treaty existing or to be concluded between Contracting States.

2. The Contracting States which do not make extradition

conditional on the existence of a treaty or reciprocity shall recognize the offence as a case for extradition as between themselves.

3. The offence shall be treated, for the purpose of extradition, as if it had been committed not only in the place in which it occurred but also in the territory:

(a) of the State of registration of the aircraft;

(b) of the State in which the aircraft lands and the alleged offender leaves the aircraft.

Article 9

1. When a person on board has unlawfully committed by force or threat thereof an act of interference, seizure, or other wrongful exercise of control of an aircraft in flight or when such an act is about to be committed, Contracting States shall take all appropriate measures to restore control of the aircraft to its lawful commander or to preserve his control of the aircraft.

2. In the cases contemplated in the preceding paragraph, the Contracting State in which the aircraft lands shall permit its passengers and crew to continue their journey as soon as practicable, and shall return the aircraft and its cargo to the persons lawfully entitled to possession.

Article 10

At the request of the Council of the International Civil Aviation Organization, each Contracting State shall furnish to that Organization as rapidly as practicable all relevant information in its possession relating to:

(a) the circumstances of the offence;

(b) the measures taken in applying Article 9 above;

(c) measures taken in respect of the alleged offender, in particular the outcome of any extradition or other legal proceedings.

Article 11

Contracting States shall, in accordance with their law, afford one another the greatest measure of assistance in connection with proceedings brought in respect of the offence.

166

Appendix 5

ICAO LEGAL COMMITTEE

Draft Convention on Unlawful Seizure of Aircraft

THE STATES PARTIES TO THIS CONVENTION
CONSIDERING that unlawful acts of seizure or exercise of control of aircraft in flight jeopardize the safety of persons and property, seriously affect the operation of international air services, and undermine the confidence of the peoples of the world in the safety of civil aviation;
CONSIDERING that the occurrence of such acts is a matter of grave concern;
CONSIDERING that for the purpose of deterring such acts, there is an urgent need to make them punishable as an offence and to provide for appropriate measures to facilitate prosecution and extradition of offenders;
CONSIDERING, in consequence, that it is necessary to adopt provisions additional to those of international agreements in force and in particular to those of the Convention signed at Tokyo on 14 September 1963 on Offences and Certain Other Acts Committed on Board Aircraft,
HAVE AGREED AS FOLLOWS:

Article 1
Any person who on board an aircraft in flight:
(a) unlawfully, by force or threat thereof, or by any other form of intimidation, seizes or exercises control of that aircraft, or attempts to perform any such act, or
(b) is an accomplice of a person who performs or attempts to perform any such act,
commits an offence (hereinafter referred to as "the offence").

Article 2

1. For the purposes of this Convention, an aircraft is considered to be in flight from the moment when power is applied for the purpose of take-off until the moment when the landing run ends.

2. This Convention shall not apply to aircraft used in military, customs or police services.

3. This Convention shall apply only if the place of take-off or the place of landing of the aircraft on board which the offence is committed is situated outside the territory of the State of registration of that aircraft.

4. In the cases mentioned in Article 5 this Convention shall not apply if the place of take-off and the place of landing of the aircraft on board which the offence is committed are situated within the territory of the same State where that State is one of those referred to in that Article.

Article 3

Each Contracting State undertakes to make the offence punishable by severe penalties.

Article 4

1. Each Contracting State shall take such measures as may be necessary to establish its jurisdiction over the offence in the following cases:

(a) when the offence is committed on board an aircraft registered in that State;

(b) when the aircraft lands in its territory with the alleged offender still on board.

2. This Convention does not exclude any criminal jurisdiction exercised in accordance with national law.

Article 5

The Contracting States which establish joint air transport operating organizations or international operating agencies, which operate aircraft which are subject to joint or international registration shall, by appropriate means, designate for each aircraft the State among them which shall exercise the jurisdiction and have the attributes of the State of registration for the purposes of this Convention and shall give notice thereof to the International Civil Aviation Organization which shall communicate the notice to all States Parties to this Convention.

Article 6

1. Upon being satisfied that the circumstances so warrant, any Contracting State in the territory of which the alleged offender is present, shall take him into custody or take other measures to ensure his presence. The custody and other measures shall be as provided in the law of that State but may only be continued for such time as is reasonably necessary to enable any criminal or extradition proceedings to be instituted.

2. Such State shall immediately make a preliminary enquiry into the facts.

3. Any person in custody pursuant to paragraph 1 shall be assisted in communicating immediately with the nearest appropriate representative of the State of which he is a national.

4. When a State, pursuant to this Article, has taken a person into custody, it shall immediately notify the State of registration of the aircraft and the State of nationality of the detained person and, if it considers it advisable, any other interested States of the fact that such person is in custody and of the circumstances which warrant his detention. The State which makes the preliminary enquiry contemplated in paragraph 2 of this Article shall promptly report its findings to the said States and shall indicate whether it intends to exercise jurisdiction.

Article 7

The Contracting State which has taken measures pursuant to Article 6, paragraph 1 shall, if it does not extradite the alleged offender, be obliged to submit the case to its competent authorities for their decision whether to prosecute him. These authorities shall take their decision in the same manner as in the case of other offences.

Article 8

1. The offence shall be deemed to be included as an extraditable offence in any extradition treaty existing between Contracting States. Contracting States undertake to include the offence as an extraditable offence in every extradition treaty to be concluded between them.

2. The Contracting States which do not make extradition conditional on the existence of a treaty shall recognize the offence as an extraditable offence between themselves subject to the conditions established by the law of the State requested to extradite.

3. The offence shall be treated, for the purpose of extradition between Contracting States, as if it had been committed not only in the place in which it occured but also in the territory:

(a) of the State of registration of the aircraft;

(b) of every State in which the aircraft lands with the alleged offender still on board.

Article 9

1. When any of the acts mentioned in Article 1 (a) has occurred or is about to occur, Contracting States shall take all appropriate measures to restore control of the aircraft to its lawful commander or to preserve his control of the aircraft.

2. In the cases contemplated in the preceding paragraph, the Contracting State in which the aircraft lands shall permit its passengers and crew to continue their journey as soon as practicable, and shall return the aircraft and its cargo to the persons lawfully entitled to possession.

Article 10

Contracting States shall, in accordance with the applicable law, afford one another the greatest measure of assistance in connection with proceedings brought in respect of the offence.

Appendix 6

THE HAGUE CONVENTION, 1970

Convention for the Suppression of Unlawful Seizure of Aircraft
(The Hague, December 16, 1970)

Preamble

THE STATES PARTIES TO THIS CONVENTION

CONSIDERING that unlawful acts of seizure or exercise of control of aircraft in flight jeopardize the safety of persons and property, seriously affect the operation of air services, and undermine the confidence of the peoples of the world in the safety of civil aviation;

CONSIDERING that the occurrence of such acts is a matter of grave concern;

CONSIDERING that, for the purpose of deterring such acts, there is an urgent need to provide appropriate measures for punishment of offenders;

HAVE AGREED AS FOLLOWS:

Article 1

Any person who on board an aircraft in flight:

(a) unlawfully, by force or threat thereof, or by any other form of intimidation, seizes, or exercises control of, that aircraft, or attempts to perform any such act, or

(b) is an accomplice of a person who performs or attempts to perform any such act

commits an offence (hereinafter referred to as "the offence").

Article 2

Each Contracting State undertakes to make the offence punishable by severe penalties.

171

Article 3

1. For the purposes of this Convention, an aircraft is considered to be in flight at any time from the moment when all its external doors are closed following embarkation until the moment when any such door is opened for disembarkation. In the case of a forced landing, the flight shall be deemed to continue until the competent authorities take over the responsibility for the aircraft and for persons and property on board.

2. This Convention shall not apply to aircraft used in military, customs or police services.

3. This Convention shall apply only if the place of take-off or the place of actual landing of the aircraft on board which the offence is committed is situated outside the territory of the State of registration of that aircraft; it shall be immaterial whether the aircraft is engaged in an international or domestic flight.

4. In the cases mentioned in Article 5, this Convention shall not apply if the place of take-off and the place of actual landing of the aircraft on board which the offence is committed are situated within the territory of the same State where that State is one of those referred to in that Article.

5. Notwithstanding paragraphs 3 and 4 of this Article, Articles 6, 7, 8 and 10 shall apply whatever the place of take-off or the place of actual landing of the aircraft, if the offender or the alleged offender is found in the territory of a State other than the State of registration of that aircraft.

Article 4

1. Each Contracting State shall take such measures as may be necessary to establish its jurisdiction over the offence and any other act of violence against passengers or crew committed by the alleged offender in connection with the offence, in the following cases:

(a) when the offence is committed on board an aircraft registered in that State;

(b) when the aircraft on board which the offence is committed lands in its territory with the alleged offender still on board;

(c) when the offence is committed on board an aircraft leased without crew to a lessee who has his principal place of business or, if the lessee has no such place of business, his permanent residence, in that State.

2. Each Contracting State shall likewise take such measures as may be necessary to establish its jurisdiction over the offence in the case where the alleged offender is present in its territory and it does not extradite him pursuant to Article 8 to any of the States mentioned in paragraph 1 of this Article.

3. This Convention does not exclude any criminal jurisdiction exercised in accordance with national law.

Article 5

The Contracting States which establish joint air transport operating organizations or international operating agencies, which operate aircraft which are subject to joint or international registration shall, by appropriate means, designate for each aircraft the State among them which shall exercise the jurisdiction and have the attributes of the State of registration for the purpose of this Convention and shall give notice thereof to the International Civil Aviation Organization which shall communicate the notice to all States Parties to this Convention.

Article 6

1. Upon being satisfied that the circumstances so warrant, any Contracting State in the territory of which the offender or the alleged offender is present, shall take him into custody or take other measures to ensure his presence. The custody and other measures shall be as provided in the law of that State but may only be continued for such time as is necessary to enable any criminal or extradition proceedings to be instituted.

2. Such State shall immediately make a preliminary enquiry into the facts.

3. Any person in custody pursuant to paragraph 1 of this Article shall be assisted in communicating immediately with the nearest appropriate representative of the State of which he is a national.

4. When a State, pursuant to this Article, has taken a person into custody, it shall immediately notify the State of regis-

tration of the aircraft, the State mentioned in Article 4, paragraph 1 *(c)*, the State of nationality of the detained person and, if it considers it advisable, any other interested States of the fact that such person is in custody and of the circumstances which warrant his detention. The State which makes the preliminary enquiry contemplated in paragraph 2 of this Article shall promptly report its findings to the said States and shall indicate whether it intends to exercise jurisdiction.

Article 7
The Contracting State in the territory of which the alleged offender is found shall, if it does not extradite him, be obliged, without exception whatsoever and whether or not the offence was committed in its territory, to submit the case to its competent authorities for the purpose of prosecution.

Those authorities shall take their decision in the same manner as in the case of any ordinary offence of a serious nature under the law of that State.

Article 8
1. The offence shall be deemed to be included as an extraditable offence in any extradition treaty existing between Contracting States. Contracting States undertake to include the offence as an extraditable offence in every extradition treaty to be concluded between them.

2. If a Contracting State which makes extradition conditional on the existence of a treaty receives a request for extradition from another Contracting State with which it has no extradition treaty, it may at its option consider this Convention as the legal basis for extradition in respect of the offence. Extradition shall be subject to the other conditions provided by the law of the requested State.

3. Contracting States which do not make extradition conditional on the existence of a treaty shall recognize the offence as an extraditable offence between themselves subject to the conditions provided by the law of the requested State.

4. The offence shall be treated, for the purpose of extradition between Contracting States, as if it had been committed not only in the place in which it occurred but also in the

174

territories of the States required to establish their jurisdiction in accordance with Article 4, paragraph 1.

Article 9

1. When any of the acts mentioned in Article 1 (a) has occurred or is about to occur, Contracting States shall take all appropriate measures to restore control of the aircraft to its lawful commander or to preserve his control of the aircraft.

2. In the cases contemplated by the preceding paragraph, any Contracting State in which the aircraft or its passengers or crew are present shall facilitate the continuation of the journey of the passengers and crew as soon as practicable, and shall without delay return the aircraft and its cargo to the persons lawfully entitled to possession.

Article 10

1. Contracting States shall afford one another the greatest measure of assistance in connection with criminal proceedings brought in respect of the offence and other acts mentioned in Article 4. The law of the State requested shall apply in all cases.

2. The provisions of paragraph 1 of this Article shall not affect obligations under any other treaty, bilateral or multilateral, which governs or will govern, in whole or in part, mutual assistance in criminal matters.

Article 11

Each Contracting State shall in accordance with its national law report to the Council of the International Civil Aviation Organization as promptly as possible any relevant information in its possession concerning:
(a) the circumstances of the offence;
(b) the action taken pursuant to Article 9;
(c) the measures taken in relation to the offender or the alleged offender, and, in particular, the results of any extradition proceedings or other legal proceedings.

Article 12

1. Any dispute between two or more Contracting States concerning the interpretation or application of this Convention which cannot be settled through negotiation, shall, at the request of one of them, be submitted to arbitration. If within six months from the date of the request for arbitration the Parties are unable to agree on the organization of the arbitration, any one of those Parties may refer the dispute to the International Court of Justice by request in conformity with the Statute of the Court.

2. Each State may at the time of signature or ratification of this Convention or accession thereto, declare that it does not consider itself bound by the preceding paragraph. The other Contracting States shall not be bound by the preceding paragraph with respect to any Contracting State having made such a reservation.

3. Any Contracting State having made a reservation in accordance with the preceding paragraph may at any time withdraw this reservation by notification to the Depositary Governments.

Article 13

1. This Convention shall be open for signature at The Hague on 16 December 1970, by States participating in the International Conference on Air Law held at The Hague from 1 to 16 December 1970 (hereinafter referred to as The Hague Conference). After 31 December 1970, the Convention shall be open to all States for signature in Moscow, London and Washington. Any State which does not sign this Convention before its entry into force in accordance with paragraph 3 of this Article may accede to it at any time.

2. This Convention shall be subject to ratification by the signatory States. Instruments of ratification and instruments of accession shall be deposited with the Governments of the Union of Soviet Socialist Republics, the United Kingdom of Great Britain and Northern Ireland, and the United States of America, which are hereby designated the Depositary Governments.

3. This Convention shall enter into force thirty days fol-

lowing the date of the deposit of instruments of ratification by ten States signatory to this Convention which participated in The Hague Conference.

4. For other States, this Convention shall enter into force on the date of entry into force of this Convention in accordance with paragraph 3 of this Article, or thirty days following the date of deposit of their instruments of ratification or accession, whichever is later.

5. The Depositary Governments shall promptly inform all signatory and acceding States of the date of each signature, the date of deposit of each instrument of ratification or accession, the date of entry into force of this Convention, and other notices.

6. As soon as this Convention comes into force, it shall be registered by the Depositary Governments pursuant to Article 102 of the Charter of the United Nations and pursuant to Article 83 of the Convention on International Civil Aviation (Chicago, 1944).

Article 14

1. Any Contracting State may denounce this Convention by written notification to the Depositary Governments.

2. Denunciation shall take effect six months following the date on which notification is received by the Depositary Governments.

In witness whereof the undersigned Plenipotentiaries, being duly authorised thereto by their Governments, have signed this Convention.

Done at The Hague, this sixteenth day of December, one thousand nine hundred and seventy, in three originals, each being drawn up in four authentic texts in the English, French, Russian and Spanish languages.

Appendix 7

ICAO LEGAL COMMITTEE

Draft Convention on Acts of Unlawful Interference against international Civil Aviation
(Other than those Covered by the Draft Convention on Unlawful Seizure of Aircraft)

Article 1
   A person commits an offence who unlawfully:
(1) intentionally commits an armed attack against the life of a person on board an aircraft in flight; or
(2) intentionally destroys or seriously damages an aircraft in service; or
(3) intentionally damages an aircraft in service with the result of endangering its safety in flight; or
(4) intentionally destroys or damages air navigation facilities with the result of endangering the safety of aircraft in flight; or
(5) intentionally commits an act of interference with the operation of aeronautical communications with the result of endangering the safety of aircraft in flight; or
(6) intentionally places on an aircraft by mail or despatching of cargo or any other means whatsoever a device or substance likely to destroy or seriously damage the aircraft in service or endanger its safety in flight; or
(7) commits any other act or omission with the intention of endangering the safety of aircraft in flight; or
(8) attempts or conspires to commit any of the above acts or omissions; or
(9) is an accomplice of a person who commits or attempts to commit any of the above acts or omissions.

Article 2

1. (a) For the purposes of this Convention, an aircraft shall be deemed to be "in service" from the moment of the beginning of its pre-flight handling until final parking at its ultimate destination in its home country.

(b) Without prejudice to paragraph 1(a), where any person has unlawfully seized or exercised control of an aircraft in flight, that aircraft shall be deemed to be in service for the entire period of unlawful seizure or exercise of control.

2. For the purposes of this Convention an aircraft shall be considered to be in flight at any time from the moment when its external doors are closed following embarkation until the moment when any such door is opened for disembarkation.

Article 3

Each Contracting State undertakes to make the offences in Article 1 punishable by severe penalties.

Article 4

This Convention shall not apply to aircraft used in military, customs or police services.

Article 5

1. Each Contracting State shall take such measures as may be necessary to establish its jurisdiction over the offences in Article 1 in the following cases:

(a) when any such offence has been committed in the territory of that State;

(b) when any such offence has been committed on board an aircraft registered in that State or against such an aircraft;

(c) when the effect of any such offence has occurred in the territory of that State.

2. Each Contracting State [shall] [may] take the necessary measures to establish its jurisdiction over the offences in Article 1 when such offences are committed on board an aircraft operated by a carrier who has his head office in that State, even though the aircraft may not be owned by the carrier.

3. This Convention does not exclude any criminal jurisdiction exercised in accordance with national law.

Article 6

1. Upon being satisfied that the circumstances so warrant, any Contracting State in the territory of which the alleged offender is present, shall take him into custody or take other measures to ensure his presence. The custody and other measures shall be as provided in the law of that State but may only be continued for such time as is reasonably necessary to enable any criminal or extradition proceedings to be instituted.

2. Such State shall immediately make a preliminary enquiry into the facts.

3. Any person in custody pursuant to paragraph 1 shall be assisted in communicating immediately with the nearest appropriate representative of the State of which he is a national.

4. When a State, pursuant to this Article, has taken a person into custody, it shall immediately notify the State of registration of the aircraft and the State of nationality of the detained person and, if it considers it advisable, any other interested States of the fact that such person is in custody and of the circumstances which warrant his detention. The State which makes the preliminary enquiry contemplated in paragraph 2 of this Article shall promptly report its findings to the said States and shall indicate whether it intends to exercise jurisdiction.

Article 7

The Contracting State which has taken measures pursuant to Article 6, paragraph 1, shall, if it does not extradite the alleged offender, be obliged to submit the case to its competent authorities for their decision whether to prosecute him. These authorities shall take their decision in the same manner as in the case of other offences.

Article 8

1. The offence shall be deemed to be included as an extraditable offence in any extradition treaty existing between Contracting States. Contracting States undertake to include the offence as an extraditable offence in every extradition treaty to be concluded between them.

2. The Contracting States which do not make extradition

conditional on the existence of a treaty shall recognize the offence as an extraditable offence between themselves subject to the conditions established by the law of the State requested to extradite.

3. The offence shall be treated, for the purpose of extradition between Contracting States, as if it had been committed not only in the place in which it occurred but also in the territory of any of the States which are bound to establish their jurisdiction over the offence in accordance with Article 5 of this Convention.

Article 9

The Contracting States which establish joint air transport operating organizations or international operating agencies, which operate aircraft which are subject to joint or international registration shall, by appropriate means, designate for each aircraft the State among them which shall exercise the jurisdiction and have the attributes of the State of registration for the purposes of this Convention and shall give notice thereof to the International Civil Aviation Organization which shall communicate the notice to all States Parties to this Convention.

Article 10

When, due to the commission of an offence in Article 1, a flight has been delayed or interrupted, the Contracting States in whose territory the aircraft or passengers or crew are located:

(a) shall take all appropriate measures to restore control of the aircraft to its lawful commander or to preserve his control of the aircraft;

(b) shall permit the passengers and crew to continue their journey as soon as practicable, and shall return the aircraft and its cargo to the persons lawfully entitled to possession.

Article 11

Contracting States shall, in accordance with the applicable law, afford one another the greatest measure of assistance in connection with proceedings brought in respect of the offences in Article 1.

Article 12

When an offence in Article 1 has been or is about to be committed, the competent authorities of the Contracting States shall, in accordance with the applicable law, furnish any relevant information in their possession to the other States concerned.

[Article 13

Upon request of the Council of the International Civil Aviation Organization, each Contracting State shall report to that Organization as rapidly as possible any relevant information in its possession concerning:
(a) the circumstances of any offence in Article 1;
(b) the action taken pursuant to Article 10;
(c) the measures taken in relation to the alleged offender, and, in particular, the result of any extradition proceedings or other legal proceedings.]

Appendix 8

ICAO LEGAL COMMITTEE

Working Paper presented by the United States delegation.
Draft Convention on Sanctions
(A Convention regarding the Safety and Security of International Civil Air Transport Services)
(LC/Working Draft No. 776, October 9, 1970)

THE PARTIES TO THIS CONVENTION
RECALLING that the Contracting States to the Convention
  on International Civil Aviation (the Chicago Convention)
  have obligated themselves to ensure the safe and orderly
  growth of international civil aviation throughout the world;
NOTING the Convention on Offences and Certain Other Acts
  Committed on Board Aircraft (the Tokyo Convention), the
  Convention on the Unlawful Seizure of Aircraft (the Unlawful Seizure Convention) and the Convention on the Unlawful Interference with Aircraft (the Unlawful Interference
  Convention);
FINDING that a heightened threat to the safety and security
  of all international civil air transport exists as a result of acts
  of unlawful seizure of aircraft involving the detention of
  passengers, crew and aircraft, contrary to the principles of
  Article 11 of the Tokyo Convention, for international
  blackmail purposes, and the destruction of such aircraft;
FINDING further that the failure of any State to take into
  custody and thereafter to extradite or prosecute, contrary
  to the principles of the Unlawful Seizure Convention or the
  Unlawful Interference Convention, any person who commits an act of unlawful seizure for international blackmail
  purposes or any person who commits an act of unlawful
  interference with an aircraft which results in damage to the

183

aircraft, or death or physical injury to passengers or crew, encourages similar unlawful acts and endangers the safety and security of all international civil air transport; and
CONCLUDING that the threat of unlawful acts of seizure and interference with civil aviation is worldwide and that consultations among States and joint action by States is required to prevent such acts and secure the safety and security of passengers, crew and aircraft;
HAVE AGREED AS FOLLOWS:

Article 1. *Definitions*
For purposes of this Convention:
(a) the term "interested State" shall mean
(i) in the event of an unlawful seizure of a civil aircraft, the State of registration of the aircraft and any State whose nationals are on board such aircraft; and
(ii) in the event of an unlawful interference with a civil aircraft, the State of registration of such aircraft, the State within the jurisdiction of which such unlawful interference took place, and, any State whose nationals are on board such aircraft; and
(b) the term "air service State" shall mean any State operating scheduled or (significant non-scheduled) international civil air service to or from a State alleged or determined to be in default under Article 2 or 3 of this Convention,
whether or not such State is a party to this Convention.

Article 2. *Determination of Detention*
A. Whenever an interested State has reason to believe that an unlawful seizure of a civil aircraft has occurred and that such aircraft, its passengers or crew are being detained, contrary to the principles of Article 11 of the Tokyo Convention, within the territory of another State for international blackmail purposes, it may
(1) notify such other State of the reasons for its belief and that it will request consultations for the purpose of obtaining a determination of its allegations in this regard unless all passengers and crew have been permitted to continue on their journey and the aircraft returned to the person lawfully en-

titled to its possession within twenty-four hours; and

(2) notify all States which it believes are interested States or air service States of its notification given pursuant to subparagraph (1) of this Article and that it requests consultations pursuant to this Convention for the purpose of obtaining a determination of its allegations.

B. Consultation shall be held at (place) and shall begin not earlier than twenty-four hours and not later than seventy-two hours following the notice given pursuant to subparagraph A(2) of this Article.

C. All interested States and air service States shall be entitled to participate and vote in consultations requested pursuant to this Article 2. A finding that all passengers and crew have not been permitted to continue on their journey or that the aircraft has not been returned to the person lawfully entitled to its possession shall be made by majority vote of the States voting, unless two-third majority of the States voting decide otherwise. Such a finding shall be considered to establish unlawful detention for international blackmail purposes contrary to the provisions of Article 11 of the Tokyo Convention (i.e., a determination of default).

Article 3. *Determination Relating to Custody, Extradition or Prosecution*

A. Whenever an interested State has reason to believe that a person who has committed either (a) an unlawful seizure of a civil aircraft for international blackmail purposes of (b) an unlawful interference with a civil aircraft that resulted in damage to the aircraft or death or physical injury to a passenger or member of the crew is within the territory of another State, and that such other State has failed (i) to take such person into immediate custody in accordance with the principles of the unlawful seizure convention or the unlawful interference convention or (ii) thereafter to extradite or prosecute such person in accordance with the principles of such conventions, it may

(1) notify such other State that it is requesting a determination, pursuant to this Convention, of its allegations in this regard;

185

(2) in accordance with the attached Annex to this Convention, request the President of the International Court of Justice to establish a five-member inquiry commission to reach findings and conclusions with respect to the allegation; and
(3) notify all States which it believes are interested States or air service States of its request for the establishment of an inquiry commission.

B. The findings and conclusions of the inquiry commission shall be final for purposes of Article 4 of this Convention.

Article 4. *Decisions on Joint Action*

A. In the event of a determination of default pursuant to Article 2, States participating in consultations shall decide as soon as possible thereafter in accordance with this Article what joint action, if any, should be taken in furtherance of the safety and security of international air service.

B. In the event the findings and conclusions of the inquiry commission determine a default of a State pursuant to Article 3, then any interested State or air service State may give notice to other such States that it requests consultations to decide what joint action, if any, should be taken. Consultations shall begin at (place) within ten days after such notice is given. All interested States and air service States shall be entitled to participate in such consultations.

C. Joint action taken pursuant to this Article may include: (1) the suspension by all air service States of authority for any carrier to operate international civil air service directly or indirectly to and from the State determined to be in default; and (2) such other measures to be taken by interested States or air service States that are intended to assure the safety and security of international civil air service to and from the State determined to be in default.

D. Each air service State shall be entitled to participate in and vote on decisions whether to take joint action referred to in subparagraph C(1) of this Article, and each air service State and each interested State shall be entitled to participate in and vote on decisions referred to in subparagraph C(2) of this Article.

E. No air service State shall be required to participate in

joint action referred to in subparagraph C(1) of this Article unless a majority of air service States present and voting agree that a particular joint action referred to therein is appropriate; and no interested State or air service State shall be required to participate in joint action referred to in subparagraph C(2) of this Article unless a majority of such States present and voting agree that a particular joint action referred to therein is appropriate.

F. A decision to take joint action made pursuant to subparagraph C(1) of this Article 4 shall be binding on all air service States, and a decision to take joint action made pursuant to subparagraph C(2) of this Article shall be binding on all air service States and interested States whether or not such a State actually participated in or voted in favour of the joint action, except that such decisions shall be recommendatory with respect to any interested State or air service State that is not a party to this Convention.

Article 5. *Modification, Suspension or Termination*

A. In the event of a decision to take joint action pursuant to Article 4, the State found in default may request consultations for the purpose of modification, suspension or termination of the joint action on the grounds that such action is no longer appropriate or necessary.

B. The States entitled to participate in consultations shall meet at (place) as soon as practicable and shall decide whether the joint action should be modified, suspended or terminated. Participation and voting during such consultations shall be determined as provided in Article 4.

Article 6. *General Provisions*

A. A State which is entitled to participate in consultations at the time of the original request for consultations under Article 2, may continue to participate and vote even though the basis for its participation has ceased to exist (such as the release of its nationals from detention).

B. Copies of notices, determinations, findings or decisions made pursuant to this Convention shall be transmitted to all States parties to the Chicago Convention.

C. The failure of one or more interested State or air service State to participate in consultations shall not affect the validity of any determinations or decisions made pursuant to this Convention.

D. A State alleged to be in default may participate in consultations and vote in determinations made under Article 2. A State determined to be in default may submit appropriate documentation and make an oral statement to the States participating in consultations, but shall not be entitled to participate in any deliberation or vote, pursuant to Articles 4 or 5 of this Convention.

Article 7. *Other International Agreements*

Suspension of authority for any carrier to operate international civil air transport services by any air service State pursuant to a decision calling for joint action under Article 4, or any other joint measures taken by interested States or air service States in accordance with a decision made under Article 4, shall be considered consistent with the object and purpose of the obligations of States parties to the Chicago Convention and shall not be considered inconsistent with any bilateral air transport agreement existing between States parties to the Chicago Convention. Contracting States undertake not to include any provisions inconsistent with the obligations of this Convention in any bilateral air transport agreement to be concluded by them.

Article 8. *Judicial or Arbitral Review*
(To be based on Article 24 of Tokyo Convention)

Article 9. *Final Clauses*
(To be discussed after agreement other articles)

ANNEX TO DRAFT CONVENTION

A. Each State party to this Convention may nominate an expert to serve on an inquiry commission. The name of such expert shall be forwarded to the President of the International Court of Justice.

B. Upon request of an interested State, the President of the

International Court of Justice shall immediately nominate five experts from the list nominated by States to serve on the inquiry commission. If the President is prevented from acting or is a national of the State requesting establishment of the commission or the State against which allegations are brought, the Vice President shall make the nominations. If the latter is prevented from acting or is a national of one of such States, the nominations shall be made by the oldest member of the Court who is not a national of such State. If practicable, one member of the inquiry commission shall be a national of the State alleged to be in default, a second member shall be a national of an interested State or an air service State, and three members one of whom shall serve as Chairman, shall be nationals of States not entitled to participate in the consultations under this Convention.

C. The inquiry commission shall set its own rules of procedure. Its findings of facts and conclusions shall be made within thirty days of its establishment, or as soon thereafter as is practicable.

D. The expenses of the inquiry commission shall be borne equally by States participating in consultations pursuant to Article 4.

Appendix 9

UNITED NATIONS SECURITY COUNCIL

Resolution on hijacking of aircraft and any other interference in international travel
(Resolution 286 (1970), September 9, 1970)

RESOLUTION 286 (1970)
Adopted by the security Council at its 1552nd Meeting, on 9 September 1970

THE SECURITY COUNCIL,

GRAVELY CONCERNED at the threat to innocent civilian lives from the hijacking of aircraft and any other interference in international travel,

APPEALS to all parties concerned for the immediate release of all passengers and crews without exception, held as a result of hijackings and other interference in international travel,

CALLS on States to take all possible legal steps to prevent further hijackings or any other interference with international civil air travel.

Appendix 10

UNITED NATIONS GENERAL ASSEMBLY

Resolution on Aerial Hijacking or interference with civil air travel
(Resolution 2645 (XXV), November 30, 1970)

RESOLUTION ADOPTED BY THE GENERAL ASSEMBLY
[on the report of the Sixth Committee (A/8176)]

2645 (XXV). *Aerial hijacking or interference with civil air travel*

THE GENERAL ASSEMBLY,

RECOGNIZING that international civil aviation is a vital link in the promotion and preservation of friendly relations among States and that its safe and orderly functioning is in the interest of all peoples,

GRAVELY CONCERNED over acts of aerial hijacking or other wrongful interference with civil air travel,

RECOGNIZING that such acts jeopardize the lives and safety of the passengers and crew and constitute a violation of their human rights,

AWARE that international civil aviation can only function properly in conditions guaranteeing the safety of its operations and the due exercise of the freedom of air travel,

ENDORSING the solemn declaration[1] of the extraordinary session of the Assembly of the International Civil Aviation Organization held at Montreal from 16 to 30 June 1970,

[1] International Civil Aviation Organization, *Resolutions adopted by the Assembly, Seventeenth Session (Extraordinary)* (Montreal, 1970), resolution A17-1.

BEARING IN MIND General Assembly resolution 2551 (XXIV) of 12 December 1969, and Security resolution 286 (1970) of 9 September 1970 adopted by consensus at the 1552nd meeting of the Council,

1. CONDEMNS, without exception whatsoever, all acts of aerial hijacking or other interference with civil air travel, whether originally national or international, through the threat or use of force, and all acts of violence which may be directed against passenger, crew and aircraft engaged in, and air navigation facilities and aeronautical communications used by, civil air transport;

2. CALLS UPON States to take all appropriate measures to deter, prevent or suppress such acts within their jurisdiction, at every stage of the execution of those acts, and to provide for the prosecution and punishment of persons who perpetrate such acts, in a manner commensurate with the gravity of those crimes, or, without prejudice to the rights and obligations of States under existing international instruments relating to the matter, for the extradition of such persons for the purpose of their prosecution and punishment;

3. DECLARES that the exploitation of unlawful seizure of aircraft for the purpose of taking hostages is to be condemned;

4. DECLARES FURTHER that the unlawful detention of passengers and crew in transit or otherwise engaged in civil air travel is to be condemned as another form of wrongful interference with free and uniterrupted air travel;

5. URGES States to the territory of which a hijacked aircraft is diverted to provide for the care and safety of its passengers and crew and to enable than to continue their journey as soon as practicable and to return the aircraft and its cargo to the persons lawfully entitled to possession;

6. INVITES States to ratify or accede to the Convention on Offences and Certain Other Acts Committed on Board Aircraft signed at Tokyo on 14 September 1963,[2] in conformity with the Convention;

7. REQUESTS concerted action on the part of States, in accordance with the Charter of the United Nations, towards

[2] United Nations, *Treaty Series,* vol. 704 (1969), No. 10106.

suppressing all acts which jeopardize the safe and orderly development of international civil air transport;

8. CALLS UPON States to take joint and separate action, in accordance with the Charter, in co-operation with the United Nations and the International Civil Aviation Organization to ensure that passengers, crew and aircraft engaged in civil aviation are not used as a means of extorting advantage of any kind;

9. URGES full support for the current efforts of the International Civil Aviation Organization towards the development and co-ordination, in accordance with its competence, of effective measures in respect of interference with civil air travel;

10. CALLS UPON States to make every possible effort to achieve a successful result at the diplomatic conference to convene at The Hague in December 1970 for the purpose of the adoption of a convention on the unlawful seizure of aircraft, so that an effective convention may be brought into force at an early date.

1914th plenary meeting,
25 November 1970

Appendix 11

COUNCIL OF EUROPE. CONSULTATIVE ASSEMBLY

Resolution 450 (1970) on air piracy
(Text adopted by the Assembly on September 18, 1970) (10th sitting)

THE ASSEMBLY,

1. Expressing indignation at the acts of terrorism and vandalism committed by some Palestinian organisations, adding to the already long list of attacks and other acts of sabotage directed against civil aircraft on the ground and in flight;

2. Recognising that these acts of hijacking, sabotage, taking of hostages and black-mailing of governments are occurring and increasing only because the terrorists and their organisations are able to use the territory of certain Arab States as a refuge, a training ground and a base for action;

3. Condemning this particularly despicable form of so-called political action as a flagrant violation of human rights, infringing the freedom of air travel—a common right of all—and a crime against humanity endangering the lives of innocent people;

4. Calling upon all governments to do their utmost to secure the immediate and simultaneous release of all hostages still held, irrespective of nationality and religion,

5. Appeals to all governments to demonstrate their determination to secure the conclusion of a convention on unlawful of aircraft which will provide for severe punishment of hijackers and black-mailers, and to take sanctions against States which become accomplices to these criminal acts.

Appendix 12

COUNCIL OF EUROPE. CONSULTATIVE ASSEMBLY

Recommendation 613 (1970) on air safety and unlawful seizure of aircraft
(Text adopted by the Assembly on September 24, 1970) (18th sitting)

THE ASSEMBLY,

1. Recalling its Recommendation 599 (1970) on air piracy adopted on 18 April 1970;

2. Welcoming Resolution (70) 23 of the Committee of Ministers, adopted on 29 June 1970), by which Council of Europe member States have been invited to take action against air piracy;

3. Deploring that the epidemic of terrorism in the air continues unabated, and that Western European States have become, to an alarming extent, the victims of such activities;

4. Noting that acts of air piracy are more and more the result of well-prepatred concerted terrorism, and that States are now exposed to the ruthless violence of highly trained and fanatical groups of terrorists;

5. Considering that, over and above the crime of air piracy, these terrorists perform even more criminal acts, such as blackmailing governments and keeping passengers as hostages;

6. Deeply concerned by the fact that as a result of this rapidly deteriorating situation, criminals who, for acts of piracy, had been condemned to long-term imprisonment by due legal process have already been released by Greece, and that other air pirates are likely to be released by Switzerland, the Federal Republic of Germany and the United Kingdom;

7. Convinced that governments which face such blackmail

are aware of the full implications of the precedents thus established which are likely to lead to an ever increasing breakdown in the rule of law;

8. Noting that organised air terrorism originates in the territory of a small number of States, and that those who are responsible for it seem to enjoy moral and financial support, and even arms' supplies from the authorities of certain States,

9. Recommends that the Committee of Ministers:

I. Adopt a resolution:

(a) calling on all nations to take immediate and energetic steps to stamp out hijacking and blackmailing of governments with hostages;

(b) inviting the United Nations General Assembly to condemn strongly the crime of air piracy, and to request in particular all the Middle East States and regional organisations such as the Arab League, the Organisation of African Unity and the Organisation of American States to condemn unreservedly all acts of unlawful interference with civil aircraft, as the Council of Europe has already done by Resolution (70) 23 of the Committee of Ministers and by Resolution 450 (1970) of the Consultative Assembly, and urging the Security Council to take the necessary steps to stamp out all acts of illegal interference with civil air traffic;

(c) urging governments of member States to resist the destruction of law by organised terrorism, and to take energetic and concerted counter-measures against unlawful pressure and blackmailing by terrorists and against States which tolerate such terrorism;

(d) urging member States to introduce and maintain stricter measures of prevention and control of air travellers and luggage at airports;

(e) inviting member States to reinforce security measures on board aircraft to protect them against hijacking and, more particularly, to consider placing armed guards on board to intervene in case of attack;

II. Establish by common agreement sanctions in the field of civil aviation such as boycotting airports or air companies and refusing landing rights to the airlines operated from States on whose territory organised terrorism in the air or hijacking is tolerated or which have refused either to extradite or severely punish offenders;

III. Invite governments of member States attending the Diplomatic Conference which will be held in The Hague in December 1970 in order to conclude a Convention on unlawful seizure of aircraft:

(a) to propose the inclusion in the Convention of severe measures for the punishment of blackmailers and ensuring that hijackers and terrorists released under duress should subsequently pay for their crimes and duly serve their legal sentence;

(b) to sign and ratify the Convention, provided it is on the lines of the draft prepared by the International Civil Aviation Organisation, and to make it clear to all States in the world that adherence to that Convention and its application in the spirit of suppression and severe punishment of all acts of unlawful interference with civil aircraft is an indispensable condition of good international relations and of co-operation.

Appendix 13

INTER-AMERICAN JURIDICAL COMMITTEE

Draft Convention on Terrorism and Kidnapping of Persons for purposes of Extortion
(Rio de Janeiro, September 26, 1970)

IN VIEW of the increasing frequency and seriousness with which acts of terrorism are occurring in this hemisphere, especially the kidnapping of persons for purposes of extortion; and

CONSIDERING that the General Assembly of the Organization, in Resolution 4 adopted at its first special session, held from June 25 through July 8, 1970, strongly condemned such acts and declared that they constitute serious common crimes characterized by flagrant violation of the most elemental principles of the security of the individual and community as well as offenses against the freedom and dignity of the individual; and

That it is advisable to establish general standards for international cooperation in the prevention and punishment of terrorism and especially of the kidnapping of persons, extortion, and other assaults against them, when such acts have international significance,

The governments of the member states of the Organization of American States

HAVE AGREED ON THE FOLLOWING:

Article 1

The contracting states undertake to cooperate mutually, by taking all the measures that they may consider effective, within their domestic legal systems, and particularly those that are set forth in this Convention, to prevent and apply punishment for acts of terrorism, especially the kidnapping of persons and extortion in connection with that crime, carried out within their respective territories, when such acts have international significance.

Article 2 (First Alternative)

Kidnapping or any other offense against the life, the person, or the freedom of a foreign diplomatic or consular agent who enjoys inviolability under international law, or a member of the family of such a person protected by that prerogative, constitutes a common crime of international significance, whatever the motive for which it was committed.

Article 2 (Second Alternative)

Kidnapping or any other offense against the life, the person, or the freedom of any person to whom the state has a duty to extend protection in accordance with international law constitutes a common crime of international significance, whatever the motive for which it was committed.

Article 3

The acts of terrorism to which this Convention refers, including the kidnapping of persons for purposes of extortion, do not constitute political offenses or common crimes connected with political offenses. Such acts shall be considered to have international significance in any of the following cases:
a. When the act is committed in the territory of a contracting state and is directed against a person or persons within the territory of another contracting state;
b. when the person or persons indicted or sentenced for such an act, perpetrated in the territory of one of the contracting states, are found within the territory of another contracting state.

Article 4

For the purposes of this Convention, an act shall be considered an act of terrorism when it is defined or expressly classified as such by the law of the state in whose territory the act was committed and by the law of the state in whose territory the person who has been indicted or sentenced for that act is located.

If the legislation of any of the contracting states, does not contain the definition or classification referred to in the preceding paragraph, for the purposes of this Convention, and regardless of the legal terminology the national laws may use to describe them, the following shall be considered to be acts of terrorism: those that produce terror or intimidation among the inhabitants of a state or sector of the inhabitants thereof and create a common threat to the life, health, physical integrity, or freedom of persons by the employment of a method or device that by its nature can cause, or does cause, great damage, a serious disturbance of public order, or a public calamity, or by the taking over, the violent seizure, or the wrecking of a ship, aircraft, or other means of collective transport.

Article 5

Persons who take part in the conception, preparation, or execution of the criminal acts mentioned in this Convention shall not be protected by the territorial or diplomatic asylum and shall be subject to extradition. In every case, the determination in this regard is to be made by the state under whose jurisdiction or protection such persons are located.

Article 6

The contracting states undertake to deliver to each other reciprocally, in accordance with the procedures established by the extradition treaties in force, or in their absence in conformity with the requirements set forth in their respective laws, the persons who are in their territory and whose extradition is requested because of their being tried for or their having been convicted of any of the criminal acts to which this Convention refers.

Article 7

If, when extradition is applicable, a state should not deliver the requested person because of some impediment, the state receiving the request shall be obligated to try the person referred to for the deed imputed to him just as if he had committed it in the territory of that state, and the said state shall inform the state that requested the extradition of the sentence handed down.

Article 8

In order to cooperate in the prevention and punishment of the acts of terrorism to which this Convention refers, the contracting states accept the following obligations:

a. To take all measures within their power to prevent the preparation of acts of terrorism that are intended to be executed in the territory of another contracting state;

b. To exchange information and to consider effective administrative measures in the matter of individual security;

c. To make provisions in their respective criminal laws regarding the criminal acts to which this Convention refers if those acts are not already covered therein;

d. To comply in the most expeditious manner with any request from another contracting state in regard to any of the criminal acts to which this Convention refers;

e. To provide for expeditious extradition, procedures in their respective laws.

Article 9

Each contracting state may, in serious and exceptional circumstances, decide whether or not it would be correct to authorize departure from its territory by, or to deport, as the case may be, any person who is detained or in prison, under the jurisdiction of that state.

The interested contracting states may reach an agreement, in cases of the specific type referred to in the preceding paragraph, regarding the legal status of the persons involved.

Article 10

This Convention shall remain open for signature by the member states of the Organization of American States, as well as by any other state that is a member of the United Nations, or any other state that may be invited to sign it by the General Assembly of the Organization of American States.

Article 11

This Convention shall be ratified by the signatory states in accordance with their respective constitutional procedures.

Article 12

The original of this Convention, the English, French, Portuguese, and Spanish texts of which are equally authentic, shall be deposited in the General Secretariat of the Organization of American States, which shall send certified copies to the signatory governments for purposes of ratification. The instruments of ratification shall be deposited in the General Secretariat of the Organization of American States, which shall notify the signatory governments of such deposit.

Article 13

This Convention shall enter into force among the states that ratify when they deposit their respective instruments of ratification.

Article 14

This Convention shall remain in force indefinitely, but may be denounced by any of the contracting states by giving notice one year in advance, after which it shall cease to be in force for the denouncing state, but shall continue to be in force for the other contracting states. The denunciation shall be transmitted to the General Secretariat of the Organization of American States, which shall notify the other contracting states thereof.

In witness whereof the undersigned plenipotentiaries, having presented their full powers, which have been found to be in due and proper form, sign this Convention on behalf of their respective governments, at the city of....................................
.................this................day of.........of the year one thousand nine hundred.................

Rio de Janeiro, September 26, 1970

Appendix 14(a)

INSTITUT DE DROIT INTERNATIONAL, EIGHTEENTH
COMMISSION ON HIJACKING OF AIRCRAFT
Edward McWhinney, *rapporteur*

Provisional Report, October, 1970

(a) Questions concerning existing law relating to Hijacking of
Aircraft, March 31st, 1970.
(Annuaire de l'Institut de Droit International, 1971, vol. II).

(1) To what extent, if at all, is the existing international law
of piracy (whether customary international law, or conventional, treaty law) applicable to the act of hijacking of an
aircraft in its contemporary manifestations?
(2) Does the Tokyo Convention of 1963, as it now
stands — assuming, of course, some more general, near universal, signature and ratification of that convention in the future — provide adequate international controls for the problem
of hijacking of aircraft? It not, then:
(*a*) should the Tokyo Convention be supplemented by some
special protocol or else by a further convention? and
(*b*) what substantive provisions should any such special protocol or further convention contain?
(3) In particular, who should have jurisdiction over the
hijacking? The State of registration of the aircraft? ; the State
in whose air space or on whose territory the hijacking occurred? : the State in whose territory the hijacked aircarft
landed? ; the individual States of nationality of the members
of the air crew and of the passengers of the hijacked aircraft?
Should such jurisdiction be concurrent, or should one or more
of the foregoing States be given primacy or priority in terms of
launching a prosecution?

(4) Should the definition of hijacking be limited to the forcible taking over or diversion of the aircraft, in flight, following upon action inside the aircraft? ; or should it also include (as recommended by IFALPA) offences committed against the aircraft, passengers and crew on board or outside the aircraft, whether in the air or on the ground?

(5) Should the international law as to hijacking include specific provisions requiring the State where the aircraft lands to apprehend the hijacker and either to prosecute him itself, or else to return him under appropriate physical restraint to any other State having jurisdiction and desirous of prosecuting the hijacker?

(6) As to requests for extradition of a hijacker to another State or States to face prosecution, should the extradition be automatic, once the request is made by a State having jurisdiction to prosecute the hijacker; or should such requests for extradition remain subject to a "political exception" in favour of *bona fide* requests for political asylum?

In other words, do you think that the right to request, and the right of a State to grant, political asylum should not be any different, as between hijackers and other species of delinquents? If not, what differentiations would you make as to claims to political asylum as a human right, advanced by, or in behalf of, hijackers?

(7) Should jurisdiction over hijackers be vested in an international tribunal or should it be left to existing national tribunals? If the latter, would it be useful to try to specify, by international convention, the scope and content of the definition of hijacking, and the minimum applicable penalties; and if so would you favour any one of the definitions so far advanced (for example the IFALPA formulation, *supra*), or the penalties provided under any existing special national laws on hijacking (for example, under the U.S. Law of 1961)?

(8) More generally, do the conventions and draft conventions take into account sufficiently all relevant general principles of international law, including *jus cogens*? If not, would you favour this Commission's attempting, itself, to elaborate a new draft convention on hijacking, or would you prefer, instead, the Commission's attempting a statement of

the *lex lata* and *lex ferenda* on the subject?

(9) Finally, do you consider that the problem of hijacking lends itself to solution by international law (whether international legislation, conventions and the like, or customary international law); or do you think, rather, that under present political conditions it can only be effectively controlled by national legislation or by the action of private, non-governmental associations and groups (IATA, IFALPA, for example)? If the latter, do you see any special problems of international law involved in any such private, non-governmental action?

Montreal, March 31st, 1970

Appendix 14(b)

INSTITUT DE DROIT INTERNATIONAL. EIGHTEENTH
COMMISSION ON HIJACKING OF AIRCRAFT
Edward McWhinney, *rapporteur*

Provisional Report, October, 1970

(b) Comments of Members of the Eighteenth Commission in
response to Questionnaire. General Summary.
(*Annuaire de l'Institut de Droit International*, 1971, vol. II).

The answers and comments made in reply to the questions
posed in Part F of the Preliminary Study indicate the principal
dilemmas for the jurist in a problem area at once so urgent in
view of the constant danger to human life and personal security, and so highly political in view of all the considerations
of state policy involved in the concrete examples today of
hijacking and the illegal diversion of aircraft generally, and in
related problems of aerial security and the protection of aircraft, whether on the ground or in the air, airports and airport
installations, and airline facilities generally, from acts of
sabotage and violence.

The *first question* concerned the nature and scope of the
existing international law concerning hijacking and the illegal
diversion of aircraft generally. The English-language term,
hijacking, perhaps because of its special historical antecedents,
has a rather more precise and limited connotation than the
French-language term, *le détournement des aéronefs*. On the
other hand, in more popular usage in both languages, the term
aerial piracy *(piraterie aérienne)* is employed as a convenient
synonym; and quite obviously hijacking has certain elements
in common with classical international law notions of piracy.
Our first question, therefore, raised the question of the extent

to which, if at all, the existing international law of piracy (whether customary or conventional, treaty law) applied to the act of hijacking an aircraft. In general, our colleagues (Messrs. *Eustathiades, Feinberg, von der Heydte, Miaja de la Muela, Salmon,* and *Verzijl*), considered the existing International Law of Piracy to be quite inapplicable to hijacking. M. *Salmon,* in particular, took note of the failure of recent ventures to enlarge the traditional notions of piracy, notably on the part of the Portuguese and the Venezuelan governments in the *Santa Maria* and the *Anzoategui* affairs respectively. On the other hand, Mr. *McDougal,* thought that the customary International Law of Piracy is capable of generic extension and does indeed apply, and that hijacking is therefore an "international" crime: and that if there be any doubt about this, a U.N. General Assembly resolution should be sought for reinforcement.

The *second question* concerned the Tokyo Convention of 1963, which came into force, finally, on December 4th, 1969, three months after the twelfth signatory State had ratified it. The question was whether the Tokyo Convention provided adequate international controls for the problem of hijacking of aircraft; and, if not, whether it should be supplemented by some special protocol or else by a further convention, and also what substantive provisions any such further measure should contain. The general reaction, Mr. Salmon perhaps apart, was that the Tokyo Convention is a quite inadequate reponse to the problem of hijacking and that a fresh start is needed (*Messrs. Eustathiades, Feinberg, von der Heydte, McDougal, Verzijl*). Mr. *Eustathiades* recorded his disappointment at the deletion from the original 1962 (Rome) draft of the Tokyo Convention, of an affirmative obligation on the part of States in whose territory a hijacked aircraft may land to punish the hijacker, which, in his view, constitutes an important *lacuna* in the law; while Mr. *Feinberg* preferred the new draft convention of March 16th, 1970, prepared by the ICAO Legal Committee, on Unlawful Seizure of Aircraft. Mr. *von der Heydte* had general doubts about the use of a protocol to a treaty to regulate a major question; and, beyond this, he felt that in the particular case of the Tokyo Convention, the addition of a protocol could slow down the process of universal ratification. Mr. von der Heydte preferred a special treaty, to deal with the employment of violence against aircraft as such, against their crew, and against the passengers.

In the *third question*, we raised the question of criminal jurisdiction over hijacking, and the question of priority in the event of there being two or more competing jurisdictions. With some individual nuances of approach, our members in general favoured universality of jurisdiction. Mr. *Feinberg*, in particular, made analogy to the application of universal jurisdiction in the case of "infractions graves" under the four Geneva Conventions of 1949; and recalling also the Institut's own resolution on "le conflit des lois pénales en matière de compétence", adopted in 1931, when the Institut pronounced itself in favour of a universal jurisdiction in the case of an infraction against the general interests protected by international law such as piracy and damage to the means of international communication. As to the issue of priority, Mr. *Eustathiades* felt this was linked to extradition, while Messrs. *Salmon* and *Verzijl* felt no need for a strict order of priority. Mr. *McDougal*, on the other hand, would give priority in jurisdiction to the State of registration of a hijacked aircraft. Mr. *von der Heydte*, for his part, distinguished between compulsory jurisdiction and optional jurisdiction; in particular, he thought that the State of registration of the aircraft and also the state in whose territory the hijacked aircraft first landed, should be obliged under international law to exercise criminal jurisdiction; while every other interested state should be capable of exercising criminal jurisdiction if it so desired.

The *fourth question* was directed to the definition of hijacking, and whether it should be limited to the forcible taking over or diversion of aircraft, in flight; or whether it should also include offences committed against the aircraft, passengers and crew on board or outside the aircraft, whether in the air or on the ground. The Commission members, on majority, clearly opted for a broader definition, and one that would include acts committed on the ground, on the basis of the need for a comprehensive treatment of the whole problem (Messrs. *Feinberg, von der Heydte, McDougal,* and *Verzijl*).

Mr. *Eustathiades*, while taking the narrower view of the ambit of the definition of hijacking, pointed to the possibilities for interpretation contained in the definition of "in flight". On the other hand, several members (Messrs. *Feinberg* and *Salmon*) noted that the question went, in part, to the mandate of the Commission; Mr. *Feinberg*, while supporting the broader definition, felt that if there were any doubt as to the Commission's jurisdiction, a ruling might be obtained from the Institut's Bureau. Mr. *von der Heydte* favoured speaking simply of the employment of violence, or the threat of employment of violence, in matters of civil air transport.

The *fifth* and *sixth* question tended to be somewhat related in the answers furnished by several members. As the *fifth* question, we asked whether the International Law as to hijacking should include specific provisions requiring the state where the aircraft lands either to prosecute the hijacker, or else to return him to any other state having jurisdiction and wanting to prosecute him. As the *sixth* question, we asked whether the extradition should be automatic, once the request had been made by a state having jurisdiction to prosecute; or whether such requests for extradition should remain subject to a "political exception" in favour of *bona fide* requests for political asylum.

To the *fifth* question, six of our members answered in the affirmative, (Messrs. *Eustathiades, Feinberg, von der Heydte, McDougal, Miaja de la Muela* and *Verzijl*). On the *sixth* question, five of the Commission members were in favour of abolishing the political exception to extradition or the claim to political asylum (Messrs. *Eustathiades, Feinberg, von der Heydte, McDougal,* and Verzijl). Mr. *Eustathiades,* saw the nature of the delict involved as favouring the elimination of the political exception to extradition, drawing analogy, here, from the 1937 Convention for the Prevention and Repression of Terrorism. Mr. *Feinberg*, in advancing a similar opinion, referred to the Institut's own resolution of 1892 elimi-nating — "des crimes les plus graves au point de vue de la morale et du droit commun, tels que l'assassinat, le meurtre, l'empoisonnement, les mutilations. . . ", from the category of political delicts; he also noted that the Genocide Convention of 1948 prescribed that Genocide and the other acts enumerated in the convention should not be considered as political crimes for purposes of extradition, and that, beyond that, the Universal Declaration of Human Rights, in Article 14, affirms that the right of asylum, cannot be invoked in the case of "prosecutions arising from non-political crimes or from acts contrary to the purposes and principles of the United Nations". Mr. *von der Heydte* considered that the power to grant asylum is limited, especially in those cases where the persons seeking asylum have violated the common interests of all the World Community; he referred here, (like Mr. Eustathiades), to the so-called "Belgian" clause concerning political outrages, which excluded the possibility of political asylum for those who had committed, or attempted to commit, an outrage against a Head-of-State, a clause, as he pointed out, that had received virtually universal acceptance (save for Great Britain, Greece, and Switzerland). In arguing for the application of a similar rule to those who committed crimes of violence against aircraft, Mr. von der Heydte referred also to the principle of proportionality, contending that the "right" in whose name those who sought asylum had violated the laws was certainly inferior to the rights of free circulation in air travel. Mr. *Salmon*, by contrast, insisted that extradition could not be automatic, and that the exceptions of political crime or of right of asylum should be respected.

In the *seventh* question, the issue was raised as to whether jurisdiction over hijackers should be vested in an international tribunal or else left to existing national tribunals, and the general opinion was that it should be left to national tribunals. Messrs. *Eustathiades* and *Feinberg* both saw merits in the abstract notion of referring jurisdiction to an international tribunal: but, taking note of the failure of the United Nations project for an International Criminal Court, were not optimistic as to the chances of such an international jurisdiction's ever being established.

In the *eighth* question, we raised the issue whether the conventions and draft conventions in this area sufficiently take into account all relevant general principles of international law, including *jus cogens*; and, if not, whether the Commission

210

itself should attempt to elaborate a new draft convention on hijacking, or else a statement of the *lex lata* and *lex ferenda* on the subject. Of those who directed themselves to this question, Mr. *Feinberg* and Mr. *McDougal* seemed to favour a declaration of clarifying principles. Mr. *Feinberg* referred specifically to the resolution on aerial piracy adopted in April, 1970, by the Consultative Assembly of the Council of Europe, asking that "aviation sanctions" be applied against any violating state. On the issue of *jus cogens*, Mr. Feinberg suggested that criminal acts directed against civil air navigation should be considered as violating the most elementary principles of humanity, morality and law; and that therefore rules regulating this matter should be counted among the "imperative rules" of international law, and thus binding also on states that refused to ratify or adhere to any convention on the subject—this in accord with the World Court's opinion on the Reservations to the Genocide Convention.

Mr. *Verzijl*, taking note of current activity in ICAO in this general field, felt that the Commission most profitably should seek to take a position on any ICAO draft conventions, or else to formulate an independent statement of what an international convention on the subject should contain, without stressing a possible distinction between *lex lata* and *lex ferenda*. Mr. *von der Heydte* thought that the Commission's task was three-fold; first, to establish the already applicable norms of international law, or *lex lata*; then, on this base, to make propositions *de lege ferenda*; and finally, to try and summarise all this by uniting the norms of *lex lata* with the propositions as to *lex ferenda* in a draft international convention. Beyond this, Mr. von der Heydte, while recognising the existence of a *jus cogens* in public international law, was not optimistic as to its contribution to this particular subject.

Finally, Mr. *Eustathiades* considered that the Commission should try to elaborate a draft convention reconciling the rules actually in force with solutions *de lege ferenda*.

As our *ninth* and final *question*, we posed the issue of the law-in-action in this area, involving the question of whether the problem could best be resolved by international law, or rather by national legislative action; and whether, indeed, it lent itself to solution more effectively by private, non-governmental action, rather than by positive law sanctions, whether international law or national law. The most direct response to this particular question, perhaps, was by Mr. *Feinberg*: he suggested that it would be highly regrettable if, in default of action by States, the control of aerial piracy were to be left to the selfhelp of private, non-governmental associations like the airline pilots, and that the duty of the Institut was to lead the way in indicating *legal* solutions. Mr. *von der Heydte* tended to share this same view, suggesting that while non-governmental action had a certain value in this area, it could only prepare the way for necessary governmental measures and never replace those measures. In Mr. von der Heydte's view, the solution of the problem was to be found in a common agreement by States which had the duty to protect the freedom of air travel.

By comparison. Mr. *McDougal*, though looking to international legislation in this field, saw a role, also, for private enforcing action. Mr. *Verzijl*, by the same token, in supporting regulation by treaty, looked also to administrative controls of a *preventive* character, at airports, suggesting that prosecution *a posteriori* is not the main concern.

Mr. *Eustathiades* and Mr. *Salmon* supported an international convention in this area. Mr. Salmon also taking specific note of the advantages of initiatives at the national, governmental level and by private, non-governmental organizations, the latter in regard especially to preventive action.

It remains only to note several more general observations raised by Commission members in their responses to the foregoing questions. Mr. *Salmon* suggested the existence of an obligation of prevention on the part of States — a duty of "due diligence" — to ensure that the aircraft of foreign companies be not made the object of hijacking attempts; he also suggested that airlines have a special duty to preserve strictly their civil character and not to proceed to the transportation of arms. Mr. *Verzijl*, for his part, raised the question of who is responsible for damage caused by hijacking; and also the question of the legal powers of state agents placed on board an aircraft with the object of controlling the conduct of passengers.

212

Mr. *von der Heydte*, for his part, submitted the following three general propositions as to the international law governing the problem:

(i) The right to freedom of movement, in so far as it is a fundamental right that is generally recognised by civilised nations, includes at the same time the right to protection against any recourse to force in the matter of air traffic.

(ii) All states are required under public international law to accord this protection not only to their own citizens but equally to every person having dealings with them in matters of air traffic, whether such a person uses an aircraft of those states' national registry; or whether he departs from one of those states' national aerodromes, or arrives there or makes a stop there; or whether he flies over the territory of those states.

(iii) To guarantee this protection, every state is obligated:

(a) to cooperate with other states to guarantee as much as possible the security of air travel;

(b) to refuse all protection and above all the right of asylum to every person who has committed or prepared an act of violence against the air crew or the passengers of an aircraft or against the aircraft itself;

(c) to punish every infringement by way of violence of the right of free circulation in air travel.

Finally, Mr. *Miaja de la Muela* felt that the general problem was to balance the necessity of a vigorous repression of acts of illegal diversion of aircraft on the one hand, with the consideration that such acts of illegal diversion constituted, as a general rule, political delicts. Mr. Miaja de la Muela also considered that the qualification of an illegal diversion of an aircraft as a political infringement should be constitutive of a presumption *iuris tantum*, and in consequence should yield in the face of contrary facts.